Praise for Run Like Duck

'Witty, funny and informative. Great for someone starting out in running!' **Dr Margot Wells**

'A hilarious tale of one man's obsession, packed with advice for runners from beginners to aspiring marathon competitors.' **Sean Conway**

'Thanks to Mark's brilliant self-deprecating humour, *Run like Duck* will have you laughing up out of the couch, into your trainers, and running a hundred miles with a smile on your face before you know it.'
Moire O'Sullivan, author of *Bump, Bike & Baby*

'This book will inspire you to stop reading and run more. Better than the Bible – if you're looking for a running book!' **David Hellard**, Bad Boy Running Podcast

'God-like, majestic, awe-inspiring are all words. Buy this book.' **Jody Raynsford**, Bad Boy Running Podcast

'I haven't read this book but how bad can it really be?'
Robbie Britton, Team GB

Mark Atkinson is a husband, father and engineer. After a lifetime of inactivity and ballooning weight, he decided at thirty-two to improve his health for the sake of his kids and tried running. He is now a member of the 100 Marathon Club and can typically be found running around his home town of Milton Keynes or searching the internet for his next race.

RUN LIKE

DUCK

Mark Atkinson

SANDSTONE PRESS

First published in Great Britain by
Sandstone Press Ltd
Dochcarty Road
Dingwall
Ross-shire
IV15 9UG
Scotland

www.sandstonepress.com

The publisher acknowledges subsidy from Creative Scotland
towards publication of this volume.

ISBN: 978-1-912240-31-9
ISBNe: 978-1-912240-32-6

Cover design by Mark Ecob
Typeset by Iolaire Typography Ltd, Newtonmore
Printed and bound by Totem, Poland

To Cloë for unwavering support through my thick and thin(ner) stages. Seldom has a wife spent longer stood in the rain waiting for a brief glimpse of a tubby husband living out a midlife crisis.

To Charlotte and Billy, hoping you one day find the interest that makes you tick and that 'sweaty, stinky Daddy' has shown when everyone and everything says you 'can't', sheer bloody-minded stubbornness will change that to 'can'.

Lastly to Dad, who gave me that stubbornness in abundance and a love for the outside.

CONTENTS

INTRODUCTION

If you're reading this and you're either a friend or relative, I'll save you having to read it all: I was fat, I started running, I got moderately good, I got carried away, the end.

Anyone else, I presume, is reading this book with an interest in starting running, or as some form of inspiration for your own running. If so, thank you for picking it up. I hope you find some of it useful and at least moderately funny; a sense of humour will be essential when you're hopping across a forest because the last puddle was deeper than expected and decided to keep your shoe.

For me, running happened largely by accident, and the course my running has taken is as much due to luck and chance discussions as any overall plan. I've somehow become a regular marathoner, dabbled with races up to 100 miles and plan to go beyond. All this is despite having very poor posture, no athletic ability and a running style that's been likened to a waddling duck, my feet pointing off into the bushes like they'd rather not be seen with me. Even more flattering is my approach to ascending hills, where I resemble a silver-backed gorilla striding off for a fight.

This is not the story of a natural athlete who turned his attention to marathons and retired on prize money and sponsorships. This is the story of a fat bloke trying to be less so. I run to avoid being fat again and to keep healthy for my family.

I have on many occasions taken the support of my wife Cloë for granted. Since walking down the aisle, she's never complained about the increasing waistline and even now seldom mentions the faint aroma of sweaty trainers coming from the boiler cupboard. She's stood at the side of far too many races trying to guess whether I need a drink, some food, or just a bloody good talking-to.

Of course the best thing Cloë has provided has been our two kids, Charlotte and Billy. It was the realisation when they were toddlers that I would need to get fit to keep up with them that kick-started all this. I'd like them to grow up thinking people who don't regularly exercise are the odd ones, not the other way around.

I want the running to stick, not gradually fade like previous attempts at gym membership, so I race to keep me running. I can be overly competitive and the desire to maintain or improve times or distance forces me to keep training.

Much like ex-smokers being some of the most

sanctimonious preachers on the evils of tobacco, I'm overly keen on boring non-runners with the myriad physical and mental benefits of putting one leg in front of the other multiple times in the pursuit of pointless and worthless shiny metal things to hang around your neck. Somewhere through my journey I started to realise people were asking me for advice and listening to my random thoughts as if I knew what I was on about. Although it was frightening, I came to accept that in many ways I did, due not to any heroic or God-given knowledge or skill but to extensive trial and error. I messed up a lot. Even when told what not to do I still did it, compelled by the same inner demon that wants you to touch anything with a 'Wet Paint' sign on it.

The engineer in me that likes to take items apart to see how they work also leads me to experiment on racing strategy, pacing, nutrition and countless other areas. I've monumentally messed up more races than I've run well but I've always learnt in the process. This prompted me to start to write some experiences down as a guide to running for the rest of us; the tubby, sweaty, last-to-be-picked-for-sports-teams. I'm also hoping to keep a copy of the book by my bedside when I'm dribbling into my soup at a nursing home to prove to the carers I wasn't always the weak, wizened, wrinkly apparition before them. I often looked far worse.

This book is therefore a combination of advice for new or aspiring runners, and a recounting of my own personal progress. Don't look at my current times and discard the book, presuming it is as relevant to you as *MasterChef* is to someone that struggles to make a sandwich without injury. I am not a natural runner and not very good at making sandwiches. Everything I've achieved, every race I've dragged myself around has been done on pure bloody-mindedness and effort. I've come a long way over the years and may one day even manage a 'Good For Age' marathon time to enter London or Boston. When I first started, even running 5k seemed laughable. Running is open to all, we all start somewhere and for most of us that is rock bottom. Or wobbly bottom in my case. As the motivational posters like to remind us 'the only person who can say no is in your head, and you don't have to listen to them'.

ACT 1

WHERE IT ALL BEGAN

1

I BLAME DAVE

Having never enjoyed running at school, I was as surprised as my friend Dave when I accepted his offer to go for a run around Furzton Lake in Milton Keynes on a wet and cold February evening. It was an awful experience, and I was undoubtedly terrible. But I kept at it.

I'm still not sure why.

Although I enjoy playing sports, I am universally bad at all of them. With little innate capacity for endurance or speed I'm not a natural sportsman. I'm slow to react and have poor coordination. As I progressed through school I was increasingly rubbish. Never being picked for the team, or only allowed on for a token five minutes, is not ideal for building experience or developing talent. The only exceptions were rugby, where my early growth and width were ideal for smacking smaller kids out the way, and badminton, where I rose to the dizzying heights of being not a complete embarrassment.

The rest of my fitness and health followed the typical adolescent and teenager arc where a love for junk food, video games and drinking led to a largely inactive lifestyle. Playing sports as an adult is tricky when you're unequivocally awful. Any team that would have accepted me would have been so bad I wouldn't have wanted to join.

Despite some initially successful forays into gym membership my weight gradually crept up and by the time I was thirty-two, I was tipping the scales at more than 100kgs, well into the fat git category.

If you've ever checked the user instructions for most home exercise equipment it's typically rated to 100kg. Over that you're in the 'too fat to help' category. Nothing like kicking a person when they're down.

With two small kids and an expanding waistline I was not unusual. Still, I realised I would have to do something. So, on the fateful day in 2011 when I was asked by Dave if I fancied going for a jog I heard my mouth saying 'Yes'.

Dave had entered for a 10k race in May and was keen to start training. I was only looking to shed enough weight to see my feet. Ironically, after too many miles and the loss of umpteen toenails, I now have feet I'd rather not see.

Like most new runners I started with a run/walk approach and gradually built up. Training on my own, I largely ran in the dark so as not to scare people with my heavy breathing, waddling, sweating mass. A stretch of footpath close to our house ran across an empty field that would eventually be filled with houses and a branch of Waitrose but, for the time being, was an illuminated, flat, deserted path going nowhere. It became my own private training ground. I'd take a slow jog over a few nights each week and then start running, aiming to reach one lamp post further than the previous visit before my burning lungs and aching legs forced me to stop and take a walking rest. It was hateful, lonely and typically wet.

Unwittingly, I was undertaking my own 'Couch to 5k' programme, pushing myself a little further and faster each time.

The only advantage of training on that isolated section of path was an easily measurable improvement each week. As an engineer I appreciated the direct feedback of information, and kept at it. I now know there are many better ways to learn to run and would recommend anyone starting the journey to look for a local beginners' class or use some of the podcasts or apps for building up distance safely (Search for 'Couch to 5k' or 'C25K'). Every new runner has to start somewhere, and club coaches have seen dozens if not hundreds of newbies, each hiding whichever part of their bodies they wished looked different, in baggy clothes. Beginners may feel intensely nervous, embarrassed and unsure whether they fit, but there is really nothing to fear. Everyone is in the same situation and the moral support they get from each other can be like a 'keep going' drug.

Back at my solo running anonymous group, I found gradual performance improvement and would run along the redway footpaths into the next grid square, turn by the church in Woughton on the Green and run back. It was mostly deserted and suited me well as I figured that, in the unlikely event of a mugger attack, I was too fat and sweaty to tackle and could sit on them until they surrendered or asphyxiated.

After a few weeks I was able to run to the church and back without stopping. It felt like a real achievement that I was now, possibly, able to outrun a fairly tired three-year-old at the weekend. I could almost hear the Olympic selection committee calling.

By chance I heard of the amazing and awesome organisation that is parkrun: free weekly timed 5k runs that originated in the UK but are now spreading across the world, having been promoted by the likes of Chris Evans and other celebrities. When I first discovered them, they seemed like an almost secret club. Every Saturday, volunteers set up and hold a 5k run, pack up and are gone without trace before most people are out of bed. They are the SAS of running events with no road closures, signage or piles of discarded bottles awaiting collection.

Dave and I decided to run the free event in Milton Keynes, both feeling slightly sceptical as it all seemed a little too good to be true. Nothing in life is free, surely? One Saturday morning we showed up with respective wives carrying and pushing the children to have a go at our first 'race'.

Anyone familiar with parkrun will know that it is a timed run and not a race but, for Dave and I, running around a course with several hundred others certainly felt like a race. After listening to the briefing, we set off with barcode in one hand and a sports drink in the other. Like most early runners I'd got into the mindset that any form of exercise must be accompanied by a sports drink. I was still to learn that there are more calories in the bottle than I was expending. Water is more than sufficient, or even no fluids at all, for such a short race in early spring in the UK climate.

The Milton Keynes parkrun course has changed more times than I can remember. Popularity has grown, and new start and finish locations have been required to cope with numbers and minimise disruption. My first run started by the hotel at Willen Lake and followed the canal before heading back to the lake up the infamous zigzags. These are a relatively minor climb by most standards but, for MK dwellers, represent a serious elevation gain since anything steeper than an underpass or drop kerb amounts to a hill.

The climb starts at around the 2k mark where a stitch forced me to take a walk break. The good nature and attitude at parkrun is such that I started running again as so many people stopped to help. I didn't want to inconvenience them any further. I finished the rest of the course well behind Dave, taking another few walk breaks as I tired.

Crossing the line, I was given another barcode on a plastic tag. Now I had two barcodes and no real idea what to do with them. Joining the scanning queue I peered anxiously forward, trying to work out what happened next. The barcode system of athlete barcode and finish token is brilliantly simple, although a little confusing at first. Once processed, our two families made a visit to the café and undid any health benefits of the run.

My first parkrun struck a chord with me. That something so great and attended by so many (at the time attendance of 200–300 seemed massive but it now stands at 500–600 most weeks) could be so unknown was surprising. Why were people paying significant sums of money on travel and entry fees to races when most had one on their doorstep every week? Why weren't people shouting about it from the roof tops? I resolved to attend every week I was able, and eventually reached the landmark achievement of running the full 5k without walking breaks.

While panting and dry heaving in the scanning queue one week I physically bumped into a local runner who (after wiping off whatever gross sweat I'd transferred) explained that she'd not only run there from home but was running back as well, covering over twice the 5k distance just for fun. To someone barely able to stand after a relatively pedestrian paced parkrun this seemed an almost suicidal idea. Sure, I was aware people ran long distances, maybe even ran marathons, but they were superhuman athletes, surely? This lady looked perfectly normal.

Maybe there was hope for me, even if I would never look normal.

Your First Run

The advice below is for average humans with no underlying health issues. If you feel this doesn't apply, check with your doctor before starting. This might sound like a cop-out but if only two people ever buy this book and both die on their first run I'm going to feel guilty, not to mention get some pretty poor reviews on Amazon from bereaved relatives.

Unlike many sports, running can be for everyone but it's worth checking medical advice. Some doctors may warn you that running is bad for your knees. That said, you know what else is bad for them? Being so unfit and large you can't even see them without a mirror.

The beautiful part of running is the simplicity. While there are countless magazines and shops trying to sell you products to do it better, easier or faster, the essence of running is that you need very little. If you're starting from zero, like many of us, then it's likely you have suitable gear to hand for your level. If you're a keen player of other sports then most of the kit can be substituted for what you have already, unless your sport is diving. No one wants to see you running around the park in your Speedo.

> FEET: Once you progress and start to increase distance it's worth investing in some proper trainers, ideally with help from a running shop that includes gait analysis. Don't let that put you off though. For the first few runs you're likely to be covering short distances relatively slowly and, with a lot of walking breaks, you can get away with whatever trainers you have kicking around the house. While specialist running socks are available, with twin skin (two layers to prevent blisters) and fancy fabrics, any socks will get you started.

LEGS: Depending on weather, any combination of shorts, yoga pants, sweat pants/jogging bottoms will do. It will take a few runs to get to know how the heat or cold affects you so don't rush to buy technical running tights as you might find them useless for all but sub-zero winter.

BUMS: Underwear is a matter of choice. Some swimming shorts will have an inner mesh for the gents and be ideal for the first runs, mirroring what's on offer in proper running shorts. Some runners go commando, most don't. Stick on your most comfy undies and you're done. Unlike in the office, no one is going to care if you have VPL. Specialist running pants can wait.

TOP HALF I: A lot of magazines will chastise runners for running without a moisture-wicking technical top. While these manmade fabrics are great for drawing sweat away from the skin and marginally reducing chafing, they're also unnecessary for beginners. Stick on a cotton tee. It may show sweat, and prolonged use might lead to the odd bit of chafing, but you're unlikely to find that an issue for a few runs. Depending on weather you may need another layer like a fleece or hoody. Stick on what makes you feel comfortable. You'll generate more heat than you expect once you get going but, for beginners, feeling too warm is less off-putting than freezing your arse off on a winter's day.

TOP HALF 2 (for the ladies): You'll need to consider sports bras, if you don't already have one. Cloë tells me these are expensive and hideously awkward. Some women have recommended doubling up on normal bras should you not be ready to brave the shops and commit your cash to an ungainly item of underwear which you will need assistance to escape from.

TIMING: There is no initial need to fork out for an expensive GPS running watch. These are fancy devices that track distance and pace and can monitor heart rate and countless other data fields, allowing you to scrutinise your run in minute detail. Don't let the lack of a watch stop you when a free running app on your phone or a normal stopwatch will do.

The only other items you might need, depending on weather and time of day, is a head torch (can be purchased from most pound shops) and hat or gloves (these don't need to be run specific). Assemble your gear from around the house and go and run a bit. Don't let the magazines and TV adverts full of 'essential' running apparatus put you off. If your ancestors could chase a gazelle in bare feet wearing a loin cloth, you can manage to get to the end of the road in trainers and tracky bottoms.

Good starting points are either to run with a friend or a local beginners' group (often free for the first few sessions). Check your local running clubs or local running shop as they normally offer courses. If, like me, you're too embarrassed to be seen huffing and puffing in public, this may seem too much but don't be put off. These courses are put on by passionate runners specifically for beginners. You will not be the biggest, slowest or sweatiest runner they've ever coached.

If you still wish to hide from humanity, then the 'Couch to 5k' programme is a great beginners' resource and available as a podcast to use on your phone or MP3 player. It's designed for the absolute beginner and is largely walking based to start with, allowing for short sections of running. These increase over the weeks in a gradual and proven manner to minimise risk of injury. You'll finish the course running a full 5k. It may seem ludicrous that you might run a whole 5k when you can barely run for the bus but trust the plan and progress will come. If any week seems too hard then repeat the previous week until comfortable and move up when ready.

Building Up To 5K

Do not increase your weekly mileage by more than 10 per cent at a time. This is to avoid injuries from any sudden jump in distance, and holds true throughout the development of a runner whether moving up to 5k or 100 miles. Other sports activity may have made you cardio-capable of running in excess of what your legs and lower body can support.

You may well hear tales of runners, such as Rob Young or Steve Way, who stumbled into running and were amazing from the start, covering marathon distances within weeks. These are the exceptions to the rule. If under the guidance of a coach or running club, or simply following the Couch to 5k, you'll be guided slowly through a natural progression.

I've gradually increased weekly mileage over the years and have been largely injury-free. Some of this is luck, as on any run or even walking to work you could twist an ankle or pull something but, overall, I believe that slow increases work.

Ultimately, the best way to improve as a runner (and to get to the point where you feel like you deserve the title 'runner') is with consistent, uninterrupted quality training. Pushing through an injury will likely see it get worse, or incur other injuries as your body compensates for a stiff calf/dodgy ankle. Ramping up the distance too fast will see you prone to injury, or too tired to perform, and your next run will be so slow and awkward you'll feel like you've taken a massive step backwards and should never have started this whole stupid hobby. Don't stress. Go home and rest. Try again next session with fresh legs and a clear head.

The First 5K – Parkrun

Most running clubs use a local parkrun as a graduation run at the end of their beginners' sessions, holding to the core values of parkrun, namely making running accessible for all. The events are free, held every Saturday at 9am, and you're seldom far from one in the UK.

The day is a big deal for first-time runners, but try and keep calm. No matter what pace you go, even if you are reduced to a walk you're still doing it. Each event has a tail runner (recently renamed tail walker to encourage more participation) that accompanies the last participant around the course for safety, irrespective of whether this is a 45-minute or one-hour walk.

Although parkrun is a run not a race, it will certainly feel like a race to first-timers. People will limber up and shed layers in anticipation of getting hot, listen to the safety and course briefing and then assemble by the start line ready for the countdown. If you have no idea of your expected finish time then start near the back as it's far better to pass people than be up front and passed by hordes of runners. Make sure you have your printed barcode (the scanners won't read a barcode from your phone) and you're good to go.

Parkruns can be as social or competitive as you want them to be. There will be runners fighting it out at the front and parents with buggies, dogs or young kids bringing up the rear.

When you cross the finish line, stay in order through the funnel to receive your finish token barcode. This isn't yours to keep; it merely has your finish position on it. The timers will have logged you so the system will know that runner 198 finished in 36 minutes. Take this and your own athlete barcode to the scanners and they'll scan both your athlete and the finish barcode, with them keeping the finish token for next week. The system now associates your name with the finish position and time and you'll be emailed your result later that day. It's a brilliantly simple way of managing the results and, barring any technical hitches, makes the run director's life easy.

At this point you can congratulate yourself on completing a 5k run, something that likely seemed impossible at the start of your journey. Parkrun can be very addictive, and the striving for a better time next week, or just to complete 50 events and earn a free tee shirt, is a strong motivator.

Some runners are happy to stick to 5k. Others wonder if they have more in them.

Running Phrases

Although I've tried keeping them to a minimum, there are some inevitable phrases included in this book (and in one case excluded):

> PB / PERSONAL BEST: To beat your previous time for a particular length race. 'I smashed out a PB on the 10k race yesterday.'

> DNF: Did Not Finish. The three letters next to your name that signify you didn't manage to make it around. Whether due to injury, illness, or missing a time cut-off for a longer event, some runners take this very badly and react with self-anger and loathing. Ultimately it really doesn't matter. Dry your eyes and try again later. If you're pushing the

distance of your races, or terrain, this will happen. Some of the more extreme ultra-distance events are designed to have a high dropout with only a handful of finishers.

DNS: Did Not Start. You entered the race, paid the fee, forgot to turn up.

DFL: Dead F*cking Last. Someone in every race is DFL so although nobody ever wants the honour, someone has to have it. A frequently heard phrase reminds runners that 'DFL is better than DNF which beats DNS.'

NEGATIVE SPLIT: Running the second half of a race slightly faster than the first half. This is meant to show supreme pace control and mental application to maintain a steady pace throughout, and push at the end for the home straight. It is the more enjoyable way to run a race but can leave you feeling you kept a bit too much back and didn't make the most of the race.

POSITIVE SPLIT: Running the second half of a race slower than the first half, typically as a result of setting off too quickly and paying the price. Some runners accept a slight slowing of pace as a sign they've given their all. If the split is too big it's likely you've gone off far too hard and suffered on the final sections.

To chick or not to chick?: 'Chicked' is commonly used in running to refer to a male runner being beaten by a female runner. There are some lesser used versions such as 'Yoofed' (to be beaten by someone far younger) or 'Olded' (by someone far more senior in years).

Some sportswear companies use the phrase so you might well be passed by a lady and as you watch her saunter past, read 'You just got chicked' on the rear of her top to rub it in.

Given the accepted figure that females are typically around 10 per cent slower than their male equivalents (generally confirmed by world records) then all things being equal, a bloke should be faster than a female runner in the same age group – except that we're not all equal. Some are better runners, train harder, or just want it more. Many runners of both sexes are just trying their best to get to the end without wearing their stomach contents down their top, and are barely aware of the gender of the hundreds streaming past.

In the first draft of this book I used chicked a few times to reference races where I'd been relatively high up the finishing list but outrun by a female. On proofreading, my loving wife pointed out that it came across as deeply sexist. It's a phrase I've seldom considered but after conversation with female runners I train with (most of whom are far better than me and beat me in most races) I decided to remove it. As they explained, the tone of the phrase is important: 'Ah man, I ran so badly I even got chicked' is derogatory while 'I was on for a podium finish until I was chicked by a runner from a rival club' is (hopefully) more a comment on the higher standard of the other runner.

2

I STILL BLAME DAVE: STEPPING UP TO 10K

After completing a few parkruns, and successfully avoiding collapse on the finish line, I improved to the point of thinking that, maybe, I could join Dave on his attempt at the BUPA London 10k. It was a daunting thought but, reflecting that I had already gone from zero to 5k, I decided it was a target worth aiming for, and duly signed up.

As an incentive to prevent myself backing out, I contacted a bowel cancer charity and asked whether I could run on its behalf. My father had recently recovered from this illness, which sadly returned a second and eventually third and very final time. Once others had put their hard-earned cash on me to complete the distance there could be no backing out.

Unfortunately, due to work and life commitments, Dave and I rarely managed to train together so were largely preparing separately towards the same goal.

We'd check in with each other for reassurance and to see if either party had come to their senses and called it off. Other than the occasional parkrun together we had no indication of the comparative progress either. He'd trounce me around the Milton Keynes parkrun but the gap was decreasing. There was the outside chance I might actually give Dave a run for his money on the day.

The jump in distance has become a common theme in my running. The engineer in me would infuriate my parents as a boy by taking stuff apart and tinkering to find out how it worked and if it could be improved – or more often than not, broken beyond all repair. The same applied to running. 5k seemed impossible but I managed it. Would 10k break me? If so, what could I improve to manage it on a subsequent attempt?

For the following months my training continued much as before. Lonely sessions in the evenings led to an attempt at a parkrun personal best on Saturday. The PBs were coming thick and fast in that early period, and I became even more determined to manage another on following weeks. Saturday couldn't come soon enough.

As race day drew nearer I started running the mile from home to the lake as a warm-up, ran the event distance then slowly shuffled back to cool down. This felt like a big jump as I was now running as a means of getting somewhere I wanted to be rather than simply completing an arduous chore. These useful miles saved parking charges, which appealed to the miser in me. Sometimes though, my optimistic approach to time got the better of me and, on more than a few occasions, I would arrive to see the tail runners disappearing into the distance knowing that I would have to chase them and that there would be no PB that day.

In April, my work took me away from home to live in a hotel. Not knowing any local running routes, I tried the dreaded treadmill in the gym. After a comedy performance that demonstrated how not to run in a straight line at consistent pace, and posed a danger to other gym users, I managed to instead complete 10k on the cross trainer for the first time. This is not equivalent to running the distance, as there is less resistance and no impact from repeatedly hitting the ground, but it was my longest period of sustained exercise for many, many years and convinced me I was ready for the big day.

Once home, I gradually lengthened my weeknight runs, still running on my own and in the dark. I didn't know any longer routes, so completed laps from our grid square into the next, back and forth until I hit the magic 10k once and, eventually twice, a week.

Training for my first 10k was now complete and I looked forward with no small amount of trepidation to race day.

BUPA London 10k – 30th May 2011

It's a measure of how seriously Dave and I took this race, our first 10k, that we travelled to London the night before and stayed in a nearby hotel (or pub with rooms, as it turned out) to ensure we didn't get caught in travel chaos and miss the start. Dave had sorted the venue, an expert at finding pubs from both his work in the brewery industry and from a misspent youth. We went out the night before with the intention of carb loading on pasta (the food of the elite runners) but had both chosen pizza (the food of the ninja turtles) instead. We'd also risked a beer before returning to the hotel for last-minute kit checks and to pin on our running numbers.

Over the years the excitement of fixing a bib to your running top fades, with the possible exception for the big events like London, but that night felt akin to hanging our stockings up for Santa. We didn't know what would happen, but we'd been looking forward to it for months. Hopefully, we'd both been good boys and St Nicholas would look out for us. Dave, being meticulous, took great care to ensure his bib was pinned perfectly level and square on his top. I mostly just stuck myself with the pins repeatedly. Taking turns to ring our loved ones for mutual reassurance we pored over the event magazine, reading and re-reading the final instructions and event layout to ensure we didn't make a mess of the whole thing.

We slept sporadically, having drunk far too many energy concoctions and too much water, and wore a path across the carpet as we rolled out of our respective beds and shuffled to the toilet to vacate overly full bladders too many times to get a decent sleep.

After a light breakfast (after all we were going to be running a whole 10k!) we rang our wives to assure them we weren't going to die in the undertaking, and made our way to the start.

The scale of the race blew us away! Ten thousand runners looks a lot different to 300 at your local parkrun.

After dropping off our kit bags and making sure we

had (more than) enough energy gels and jelly beans and were (massively over) hydrated, we went to our respective starting pens. Dave had estimated a finish time around 55 minutes so was somewhere in the top half. When I signed up I wasn't even sure how far 10k was, so had guessed a time somewhere around 1h 30. Training runs had since shown that I was likely to be under an hour, but it was too late to change when I realised.

Regret only increased when I found my pen and realised that I would have difficulty physically getting inside. It wasn't the number of runners; it was the size of them. Still a fat lad myself, I looked on the verge of starvation compared to my pen-mates.

Not wanting to be judgemental, I struck up a few conversations and learned that some of them had trained. A bit. From an unscientific straw poll, it seemed completing a parkrun at much more than a walk would be high preparation for this particular pen.

If this sounds unduly harsh, let me say I genuinely applaud anyone who gets themselves off the sofa and starts running. My own early painful, embarrassing efforts pale beside the dedication shown by these people. Not to mention the mockery and finger-pointing many had likely endured, as white van drivers love to honk their horns and shout abuse at runners.

My personal aim, to finish under an hour, would be a tall order from so far back. I sharpened my elbows and squeezed to the front, hoping my rapidly (re)filling bladder would hold out.

Over the tannoy we heard the elite pen set off, with the

world famous Mo Farah leading the field. Gradually the other pens were released until it was our turn. I crossed the starting mat, started my watch and began to run or, at least, tried to. An impenetrable wall of people moved slowly forward in front of me, many walking hand in hand in solidarity, sharing the triumph of personal hurdles overcome to get to the start of the race. It was a great moment for them, but a frustrating one for me as I looked for a gap.

After around 1k I had moved far enough forward to see the road under my feet, and to where the general forward motion of those around me could be described as at least jogging. Working as hard as I could, I cut through and darted around runners like a motorcyclist with a death wish on a busy motorway.

Feeling in need of a boost, I opened my energy jelly beans at about halfway. The packet split, the contents were strewn across the road, and I feared I might have manufactured a disaster of runners skating and slipping on my unintentional booby trap. Fortunately, the sweets were trampled harmlessly into the tarmac.

Grabbing a sports drink at the next aid station, I ran along the iconic Mall to finish in 53m 40s with my bladder stretched to bursting. Dave had finished well ahead due to the differing start pens, but with a marginally slower time. He'd started this unlikely journey from a far better level of fitness than me but I'd somehow overcome the detrimental effects of countless cheese-burgers, and caught up. Other than the occasional game of golf before we became fathers, this was the first time we'd gone against each other and I'd come out ahead. If

Dave was disappointed he hid it well and we celebrated overcoming the seemingly impossible together.

My victory started the cogs in my head turning. Maybe running was something I could be good at?

After the obligatory medal photos all that was left to do was ring the families to assure them we had, as promised, survived. My first proper race was done.

What had seemed a ridiculous distance when I signed up, had passed without incident but, crucially, without giving me the chance to push myself. For Dave this was probably the highlight of his running career. We ran one more race together in autumn of the same year, a local 10k run over the hills of Luton. Dave had run sporadically in between. I'd not let up on the training and the difference was telling as I finished even further ahead than in London.

I was itching to see what more my fat little legs could do and what it would take to break them.

Running shoes

By this stage you've done enough runs to feel you're going to keep at it. It probably isn't 'fun' yet but neither is it torture. It's now worthwhile forking out some cash. Although running is inherently cheap and can be done in whatever you have to hand, getting a decent pair of shoes is one of the few areas you shouldn't skimp or choose poorly. They don't have to be expensive. Aim for suitable and sufficient.

Best tip is to visit your local running specialist. Most

have treadmills or, at least, areas of the shop you can run down while trained staff assess your style. Don't be put off by being a newbie who has no clue, most people in there for analysis are new runners as experienced runners know what they need. The staff will also throw around jargon which sounds more complicated than it is. Essentially the terms are used to describe how your foot lands and pushes off with each stride. By assessing how you run, they can pick the best shoe to aid your training.

For most of us, each stride will land towards the outside of the heel, roll inwards and then push off from the front of the foot, ideally with most power going through the bigger toes.

PRONATION is a measure of how much your foot rolls inward during a landing after initially making contact towards the outside edge of the heel. A normal pronation is around a 15 per cent roll and allows your foot and ankle to take the body weight imposed. As you leave the ground for the next stride you will be pushing off from the front of the foot.

OVERPRONATION is when the ankle rolls further inwards. The foot and ankle are less able to take the body weight and the loading isn't absorbed as well.

UNDERPRONATION again starts with the outside of the heel making contact first, but with insufficient inward roll. This focuses the impact on a smaller area of the foot and the pushing off is done less effectively as it's from the outside edge of the foot (your smaller toes).

How much you pronate is often influenced by your foot arch. A flat-footed runner is more likely to overpronate while someone with a very high arch will typically under-pronate.

Those with normal- or underpronation are best suited to a neutral shoe, sometimes referred to as a cushioned shoe. Overpronation will require a stability, support or motion control shoe. Once you've been assessed for running style you can narrow down your search. Some shoe styles are made in several versions to cater for pronation. Some are made specifically for one style.

Another possibility is when the runner lands too heavily on a heel with it too far in front of the body (over striding). This is termed heel strike and jars the body while marginally applying the brakes, so the running motion becomes a constant braking and accelerating. Elite runners have a more fluid motion where their feet move more like the motion of cyclists with minimal or no heel strike and braking effect. If you later adopt the natural or barefoot method you'll be aiming for a forefoot landing.

Other factors to consider are your weight. If over 12–13 stone you're likely going to need something cushioned. How much will depend on your mileage and running style. For short races a minimal or racing flat might be suitable, but running over a 10k or half marathon (HM) would often need some more cushioning.

Once you've had the assessment they'll pick out the

best shoe and you'll likely wince at the cost. There's no reason to pay a lot for the ideal shoe but (by complete coincidence) the only suitable shoes in stock and in your size will be close to the price of a romantic dinner for two. You have the option of buying them or remembering the size and style and checking online. If it's a small independent shop that's gone out of their way to assist, then it's worth supporting them and maybe buying subsequent pairs online to save pennies.

Most running shops give discounts for members of running clubs, so always ask before parting with your cash.

As you progress, it is possible that your feet and style will change, so it's recommended to revisit if you find you no longer get along with your trainers. It might be they're worn and need replacement; it could be you need something different. After 30 years of being flat-footed, running has given me an instep and an arch I never had.

A lot of manufacturers will say that trainers will only be suitable for 500 miles of use. Of course, they have your best interests at heart and certainly aren't trying to make you replace trainers more regularly. Honest.

How many miles you actually get will vary a lot depending on your running form, frequency of use and style of the shoe. If you need a heavily cushioned shoe, you'll notice a lot sooner if this is fading than on a more minimalist shoe with little to wear. Some of the running apps allow you to record which shoe was used for each run so the more scientific of you can monitor exactly how close to replacement each pair is. Some of mine have lasted nearly 1,000 miles, some feel decidedly gone by 400. Rotating a couple of pairs of shoes so they have a rest between uses can help.

It's worth keeping a tired pair in the cupboard in case you ever do an obstacle race or similar as typically these involve a lot of water and mud. You can bin the shoes after the event rather the stink the car or house out.

5k to 10k

If you've mastered a 5k then the increase to 10k is within your grasp and less of a jump than that of the sedentary primate you used to be completing the local parkrun, although it may not seem that way. Programmes available from running clubs and magazines are merely an extension of what has gone before, with a number of runs a week aimed to increase fitness, speed and endurance. Most clubs have sessions aimed at this increase but, if on your own, you can start by adding a run on before or after parkrun. My preference is before, as it's too tempting to go to the coffee shop with your mates after.

Training Sessions

You may find the programmes and coaches start dropping in a few technical phrases around your sessions, but they aren't as mystifying as they may at first sound. All these runs will have warm-up and cool-down sessions to help avoid injury. As a beginner you've been working on increasing general fitness with improvements in speed and endurance. More specific sessions will target one or both, or focus on technique. All should follow proper warm-up routines.

EASY RUN: The base run of your workout, taken at a pace that allows you to hold a conversation with a running partner but with the main aim of getting time on your feet. Four miles gentle running in an hour will get you used to continued effort for a longer period than your usual 5k without placing undue strain on your legs, leaving you fresh for a tempo run in the next session.

TEMPO RUN: This is a sustained period of fairly high effort just outside your comfort zone. You should be aware of your breathing, that it's not rasping, and be able to share a few short words with other runners but not hold a conversation. If you can discuss in detail what you saw on TV last night you're too slow. If you can't manage more than a word you're too fast. Although judging effort based on talking may appear crude it is more accurate than an absolute pace as it allows for fitness, weather, wind, terrain etc.

INTERVAL RUNS: The run is broken into short sections of hard effort with recovery sections in between. The goal is to increase the overall pace you can sustain by repeating periods of fast running. These sections should be run sufficiently hard to make breathing an effort. Other than a grunt you shouldn't be able to talk. Ideally the intervals should be consistently paced throughout, and recovery sections should avoid walking or standing, more of a slow jog to aid recovery and build strength.

FARTLEK WORKOUTS: Named from the Swedish for 'speed play' these are basically runs broken up into sections of easy and moderate to hard (fast) efforts. These can be done on your own (run fast to the next tree then slow until the bridge) but are easier as part of a group.

HILL SESSIONS: Essentially, these mean running up and down a hill for a given number of repeats, or times, to build leg strength and allow you to run with a quick cadence (how fast your feet turn over). Some sessions focus on running hard up the hills and easy down, some the other way to increase speed and teach technique for descending. If you train somewhere predominantly flat but are looking to run a hilly 10k, these sessions are useful mental preparation. Very steep hills can reduce your run to a walk. Don't see it as failure and just get over it, both the hill and the feeling.

3

13.1 MILES AIN'T HALF OF ANYTHING

Having 'mastered' the 10k, I made the next step on what I now realise was the slippery slope towards marathon distance. Maybe 13 miles would be the distance that broke me?

Flicking through our local free paper I noted a half marathon was coming up in July, in aid of the National Society for the Prevention of Cruelty to Children (NSPCC). I signed up and started buying running magazines, looking for advice and tips on training. After a few months you notice the same tried-and-tested articles being regurgitated on an annual basis. For a novice runner though, they become a sort of bible of advice and guidance.

I found a training programme that promised under two hours for a half marathon, pinned it to the study wall and, in a practice adopted by countless runners across the world, ticked off each session once done. By not looking too far ahead I avoided being intimidated by the increasing distance and pace of later weeks.

Although now a regular runner, I still hadn't plucked up the courage to join a club and benefit from their advice and camaraderie. Dave had scratched his running itch by completing the two 10k races with me and had returned to his natural habitat of the ice rink where he attempts to play hockey while breaking the fewest number of bones possible. We occasionally discuss running but my interest has taking me beyond casual enthusiast to full-on obsession.

Abandoned by the man who'd started the whole silly journey, I was back on my own, venturing further afield on my runs and seeing some parts of Milton Keynes I'd only previously driven past. Following the programme from the magazine meant I could build in a controlled manner, with the long run increasing in distance for a few weeks before stepping back, then increasing again. This process allows the body to adapt but also recover, slowly building a solid foundation to make the next increase in race distance.

Most training programmes for a half marathon are 10–16 weeks in duration and assume a base level of running ability typically capable of achieving 10–15 miles per week and around 10k or 6.2 miles as a longest run at the start. As with anything in life, it's worth building slowly.

Training plans also vary in ambition. Some are simply to get your body able to cover the 13.1 miles, others are geared towards target times, and incorporate a lot of pace specific work. While it's good to have a finish time in mind, for a first attempt, just completing the event is achievement enough. Don't put undue pressure on yourself by setting a hard target, anything under which will be deemed a personal failure. Running is meant to be fun. Remember that when you find chafing in your pants area at mile eight.

NSPCC Half Marathon – July 2011

Just over six months after I started running, Cloë dropped me off for my first half marathon. 13.1 miles: more than four back-to-back parkruns. The event in Milton Keynes started on school playing fields and winding its way out and back along the redways and pedestrianised former railways. The entrants were a mixture of hardened 'proper' running types through to fancy dress runners, all of whom looked far more capable of this than me. What had I been thinking? I consoled myself that whatever happened I was doing my bit for charity, and put a brave face on.

Although not on the scale of the BUPA London 10k, this still felt like a sizeable event as 1,600 runners gathered in the morning sunshine. For someone used to running in the evenings, a daytime half marathon in July was intimidating. Would I manage in the heat of the British summer? How much fluid should I drink? Would my kit rub somewhere it previously hadn't?

After dropping off my bag and taking part in the Zumba warm-up we assembled in the car park in zones according to expected finishing times. Based on times for 10k I was aiming for two hours.

If you're running a race and worried about time, many websites supply a pace band for you to wear. This is a simple paper band for your wrist with elapsed time targets for each mile or kilometre to reach your target time for the distance. These work best on events with mile markers along the course when all you need is a stopwatch to record time. There is no need for expensive GPS watches or to run with your phone.

Standing in the start pen I felt very out of my depth, assuming most runners were more experienced and better than me. Electing not to run with headphones, I plodded around the course with just my wheezy breath for accompaniment. For the first time I was wearing a hydration belt like a 'proper' runner. I was to learn the hard way that these are just another gimmick: an unappealing combination of Batman's utility belt and the miniscule drinking bottles used for gerbils, they are sold as the answer to all hydration issues. In most races though, water stops are frequent. If you're ever in a situation where a thimbleful of water is the difference between life and death you may have gone seriously off course and ended up in the Serengeti.

The half marathon route was largely flat, and I kept to pace. Seeing my family and parents at a couple of points en route, I was able to dispose of the pointless bottles to lighten the load. As the miles progressed my legs became increasingly heavy and I began to slow, with runners passing me at regular intervals. I managed to maintain my intended overall pace, although I had gone off a little too fast. I came into the final section anxious to finish. The route takes a final loop of the sports field and around a building, passing from road to fields by stepping up onto the kerb. This may seem minor, but after 13 miles I wasn't sure my legs would allow me to clear the vertigo-inspiring kerb. It felt like my trainers brushed it as I heaved my blistered feet up and over, onto the final stretch.

I wanted to smile and look composed for the finish line photos but that was well beyond me. My finish line photos show a confident athletic fella cruising to glory. Unfortunately that's someone else and I'm the hunched, wrecked, sweat-soaked man beside him. Coming down the finish funnel I was relieved to find myself still under two hours and, in fact, crossed the line in 1h58, nicely under my two-hour target on one of the few races I've ever paced well.

The banana provided at the finish line was as appetising as Styrofoam and I jerkily strutted off to find my family, knowing that if I sat down I might not make it back up.

My reward for my first half marathon, besides a medal and a manky banana, was a massive breakfast buffet cooked by Cloë. Fairly soon afterwards, I began to feel surprisingly well. I'd done the unthinkable and run a half marathon. It hadn't broken me. How much faster could I go at the next attempt?

Run to the Beat Half Marathon – September 2011

This was my second half marathon, coming two months after my first half in July. The entry fee was rather steep but, as it was a biggish event, I wasn't too bothered. Sponsored by Nike, it sent out running tops with the bib number already printed on, and a separate chip for your shoe. The tops made everyone look the same, which may have been good for photos and the sponsors but made it hard to pick out individuals.

The start was by the O2 centre (what was the Millennium Dome), which is not the easiest place to reach on a Sunday morning. This was easily the biggest event I'd run, with over 10,000 entries, and the logistics must have been a tremendous challenge for the organisers. The start pens were spread out in car parks and open spaces around the O2 to mitigate crowd density. Again running to raise funds for Beating Bowel Cancer, I was one of the few not in the event top, and stood out in a sea of purple tees – not a very masculine colour, several men commented, obviously feeling that their testosterone and full beards were insufficient to overcome such a 'girly' top.

I was resplendent in my white and red vest for 'Beating Bowel Cancer'. True to most charity tops, it was cheaply made to keep much-needed funds for the cause. Every seam was a razor-sharp source of anguish when worn. No pain, no gain, I suppose.

After dropping my bags, I joined the pen, again wearing the pointless hydration belt, possibly as some sort of security blanket. At least it would be handy if I came across a thirsty field mouse. Fifteen minutes before the start I was busting for a wee and, due to a lack of convenient trees, jumped the barrier and legged it to a distant portaloo. Last-minute loo breaks are a constant fear for runners. Everyone drinks too much the morning of a big event, leading to countless toilet stops on route. Then you join your pen and realise there are no toilets and need to go again. The dilemma of waiting for the start of the race and using a portaloo on route, losing precious time, or leaving the pen and missing the start of the race is a real one.

Back in the pen, with minutes to go, I noted hundreds of runners with their drop bags around their shoulders racing for the baggage tent. Either the tube had suffered issues or they had underestimated how much prep time a big event needs.

The event was billed as a 'music half marathon' with DJs, street bands and entertainment en route, so I was surprised by how many runners wore headphones and largely missed the event's main selling point.

Eventually we set off with me hoping for a fantastic experience, like a mini London Marathon. However, the route was largely uninteresting, for the most part following nondescript roads through housing and industrial/retail parks. An early section took in some playing fields and grassed areas where we were forced to bunch up and almost walk through a narrow gap in the fence. Had I not been following thousands of others, I would have questioned whether this was the correct route.

The music sites were more spread out than expected and the accompaniment was less than seamless, more akin to brief moments of noise interspersed by the marching feet of silent runners passing closed sofa shops in near silence. Having had a very relaxed experience at MK, I'd planned to run this one faster and was pacing for sub 1h50m but, by halfway, was starting to flag in the heat, and my cheap charity top was doing its best to rub my nipples clean off.

Coming up a small hill we heard an ambulance approaching from behind and, as one, moved to the left to let it past, except for a few runners with headphones, who were completely oblivious to the flashing blue lights and wailing sirens. Presumably they thought it was sound effects from an unusual remix of whatever track they were enjoying. Eventually, other runners were forced to pull them to one side. I watched as the ambulance slowly progressed, repeatedly being held up by selfish idiots who placed their musical entertainment higher than medical aid reaching a needy person.

Headphones in big races have become a real bugbear of mine and I'm glad the recent changes to the UKA rules have effectively banned them from most road races. They're fine for smaller events, especially those of a longer duration when you might feel the need for company. However, if you're insistent on wearing them for events like the London Marathon you really are missing out on experience and should probably not enter the ballot. Let someone who will enjoy it have the spot. Otherwise it's akin to getting tickets to a sold-out play or musical and bringing a book. Rant over.

At around ten miles my pace slowed and 1h50m became doubtful. The few music acts were more annoying than motivating by this stage, and I'd failed to see either Cloë or my father-in-law, Tony, in the dense crowds. I needed something to spur me on and a friendly face would have helped. Every barrier seemed to be a press of faces all peering for that one runner they've come to see. None of them were the faces I was looking for.

I'd neglected to write my name on my top for spectators to call out. It was an omission that denied me the encouragement of strangers and I couldn't see anyone that wasn't. I'd made a hash of agreeing a cheering point with Cloë or Tony in advance, which is something worth thinking about when organising for big events.

Happily, they did find me just before the finish line and the support spurred me to 1h55m.

The medal was pretty good but otherwise the event had been mostly disappointing and no more scenic, enjoyable or accompanied by music than the small-scale half marathon in MK. That had been organised to raise funds for NSPCC, while this one left me with the impression of being a purely moneymaking, soulless affair.

My second HM was done, a little more slowly than intended but, overall, I was content with my time. With no real issues, other than the loss of my nipples, my improvement in running over the previous eight months was pleasing. I started to wonder what else I could do. Both half marathons had failed to break me, maybe I could go further?

Note: In subsequent years the Run to the Beat suffered more issues and had some very bad PR due to overcrowding and poor routes, including reoccurrence of the narrowing of some sections, to such an extent that runners were forced to become walkers or even bystanders while waiting for space to run. It was eventually ended and replaced with a 10k run, under new management and unconnected to the previous event but still using the 'Run to the Beat' nomenclature.

Controlled Discomfort (not pain)

One of the hardest mental barriers to overcome is that, for much of the time, especially for new runners, running is not comfortable. We may have evolved to be ideally suited for the task, but it's seldom entirely pleasant and this feeling of discomfort is increasingly unusual for Westerners. We wake up in a comfy bed in a heated home and have a warm shower before popping downstairs for a choice of breakfast. When pleasantly full we jump into our air-conditioned cars to drive over smooth roads to our climate-controlled offices, where we work at ergonomically designed desks before repeating the journey home and curling up on the sofa with a choice of thousands of movies and a smorgasbord of dinner options. The Wi-Fi signal dropping out is probably the closest we get to real inconvenience.

To abandon the conveniences of life and pound tired legs over hard concrete is a perverse concept to a society dedicated to making life easier. When you don't even need to leave your car to pick up a coffee, running in the rain at a speed far less than a car towards no specific destination is a shock to the system. For some of us though, this is reason enough to run. Life is too comfortable, and they'd rather stand at the top of a hill with their chest pounding than be sat at the bottom sipping a latte and wondering what the view is like.

Getting used to the controlled discomfort of running takes time. If your sofa spring started jabbing you in the bum you'd get up and move or find a cushion, you wouldn't endure it to build character. The level at which this discomfort kicks in will vary as you progress, but however much you improve will always be present somewhere. Celebrate it. Pain should be avoided but being able to run when it's not comfortable can make you feel alive and is an indication that you're giving your body a good workout and improving as a runner. You won't beat last week's parkrun time without pushing harder.

Weight Loss and Running

For many new runners (myself included) running is not only an attempt to get active but also to shed some weight. According to the NHS website, in 2017, 24.8 per cent of adults were obese and 61.7 per cent either overweight or obese so there is certainly a need to tackle the issue.

At the risk of being controversial, I'd say that running is probably not the best weight loss approach. An active varied lifestyle with a decent diet and portion control will likely yield better results, but personally I'd rather run ten miles than give up pizza.

If you are aiming to lose weight then be mindful of how much you wish to lose, whether this is healthy, and of the calories used in running. The rate of calories used per mile will vary with pace, weight and course or terrain. Some runners are naturally more efficient for the same pace so will burn less, but 100 calories per mile is a handy estimate.

A 90kg male running a 10–12-minute mile can burn close to 150 calories or the equivalent of a typical 500ml sports drink. Neck a whole bottle at your parkrun and you've put back in a third to half of the calories burnt. Treat yourself to a Caffè Mocha on the way home (290 calories) and you've just undone all the good work and likely added calories. That's fine if you're a good weight or going to be sensible for the rest of the day but if you're planning to reward yourself with a non-stop stream of junk food and biscuits don't be surprised if you gain weight.

Gels (the little tubes of slime that manufacturers insist are the best fuel for long runs) are typically around 100 calories and some recommend taking them as frequently as every 20 minutes. Over a five-hour marathon that's around 1,400 calories plus any additional from sports drink or jelly babies. You're well on the way to replacing the 2,600–3,000 calories lost. Add in a big pre-race breakfast for fuel and a slap-up lunch to celebrate, and your most active day of the year could be your worst in terms of net calories.

Be mindful of what you eat, track it on one of the apps if necessary, and compare with what you've burnt. It's not unusual for me to have exceeded my calorie allowance by lunchtime and need to go for a run to earn some back before dinner.

For more accurate tracking of calories while exercising then a heart rate monitor (HRM) with an app or GPS watch helps, assuming you've set height and weight correctly. Without a HRM Garmin estimates I'm getting through close to 4,000 calories on a marathon. With the HRM it's down to 2,500–2,800.

What you eat can be a minefield and even nutrition experts can't agree on what levels of fat, carbohydrates and sugars are best for a healthy and extended life. Have a read around if it's something you're interested in. Low Carb/High Fat diets are attracting attention as people ditch processed foods and sugars for the slabs of meat and butter/cheese of generations ago. We could probably all eat better but starting a new fitness regime and making radical changes to diet at the same time is probably not ideal.

4

MARATHON MAN

First Marathon – Luton 20th November 2011

Having completed my first half marathon in July, and with another booked for late September, I was feeling pretty good about my running. No more was I the fat sweaty mess plodding at the back. I was able to pace myself, keep a goal in mind and come in under two hours. I'd gone from zero to half marathon in six months so decided that doubling the distance would be no big deal. So, on 1st September 2011 I signed up for the Luton Marathon of that November. It wasn't the most prestigious event to run as my one and only (or so I thought) marathon, having only 500 entrants, no TV coverage or cheering crowds but it was local so why not?

The attraction of the marathon distance is huge. Even ardent armchair athletes have watched some of the London Marathon, if only to spot their favourite celebs or laugh at the fancy dress runners doing something inconceivable to raise money for a cause. Once you start running yourself it's inevitable that the 26.2 mile distance will come up in conversation: 'Oh, you're a runner, have you even run a marathon?' These all combine in the back of the mind to make otherwise sane people consider running further than most of us drive to work.

It's important not to understate just how far that distance is. 26.2 miles is a long way. It requires preparation. You need to condition your body not just for the distance but also the long duration. Undertaking any activity for more than five or six hours should not be taken lightly.

Unfortunately I was unaware – or wilfully ignorant – of most of this. Having finished my second half marathon, I should have gone back to training and increased the distance, but I didn't. Running on my own for long distances just wasn't appealing. I kept finding excuses or running to and from parkrun and hoping a hard 3.1 miles in the middle would make up for the lack of mileage.

In early November I ran the Marlow Half Marathon as a training run, aiming to complete it at what I hoped was marathon pace, and finished just under 2h10m. My good friend Scott, who'd come along to spectate, asked if I always ran so oddly. Apparently, I crossed the line running sideways like a crab. My running form has never been anything to boast about. Despite his derisive comment though, I finished, feeling relaxed and confident that a 4h30m marathon was possible, and I could expect to finish well within the five-hour cut-off for the event. Sure I'd only covered 13.1 miles, but the same again wouldn't be that much harder, surely?

Two weeks before the big day, a few ex-runners and colleagues were politely (and eventually less so) insisting that I do at least one run, close to 20 miles, prior to race day. After checking my diary I found I had one evening free where the family would be away for the night. I went out on a cold autumnal evening run for three hours. The first two hours went well and I covered half marathon distance comfortably. Running was easy, what was all the fuss about? Then it took a turn for the worse: my legs cramped, I used more fluid than expected and had to stop at a corner shop, offering up my sweaty emergency £5 note in exchange for a sports drink. As the weather got colder and wetter I got slower and eventually dragged myself home having covered a little over 16 miles. The longest distance I'd ever run had broken me and I'd still have another ten to go on race day.

Several days later I regained the proper use of my legs. It was now too close to the big day for another long run so I focused on short runs to make sure the legs were working. The night before the marathon I could barely sleep for excitement and nerves. I then worried that the lack of sleep would have a negative effect on race day. This cycle continued through the night. Tomorrow I would either finish the day a marathon runner, or have finally found something that broke me.

Race Day

Waking early, I put on my tried-and-tested kit, but with another layer on top as it felt cold, and ate the porridge that all the magazines advise is essential. In comparison to the awful Nike Half Marathon it was not a big event, with only around 500 runners, but it was a well-organised affair. After multiple toilet trips to make sure I wouldn't need to stop for a wee mid-race, I dropped my bag and assembled on the grass outside the sports hall. Despite the issues on my long run, I felt confident about the three laps and intended to complete each with metronomic precision at 1h30m for a 4h30m finish.

Some advice from the Marathon Talk podcast was in my head, comparing a marathon to a pebble on the beach. At the start of the race the tide moves out and runners will go out too hard and pass you. At the mid-point the tide will turn, and you'll reel them back in as they suffer from their ambitious start. That was the plan in my head as the starting pistol fired. I had never heard one before that day. Out I trotted on my first marathon!

Luton is not particularly scenic so neither is its marathon. Growing up in Dunstable, we used to joke that Luton only existed to make living in Dunstable feel less bad in comparison. The first and last section of each lap of the course ran past run-down tower blocks before heading into the countryside.

Despite my reservations, the locals were supportive and a great boost to morale.

I was swept along by the other runners and easily achieved a 1h20m first lap. Maybe this was my marathon pace? Ten minutes quicker than planned wasn't significant, surely? It felt easy, but could I hold it for three laps and have a marathon debut of four hours? These thoughts were soon vanquished as my legs began to slow. The pace proved too fast on the second lap, slowing me to 1h40m. Reassuring myself that this still gave me 1h30m to achieve target time all I needed to do was speed up a bit. Easy. I did the best I could to drink from the aid station cups (a skill I have never mastered) and set off for glory. Or, as it turned out, agony.

Every mile was slower than the last. Energy beans and gels were not helping and were hard to keep down. My stomach made alarming noises and I felt that an excess of gels and fluids were about to make a bid for freedom. This slowed me to a jog, but I stopped worrying about stomach issues around mile 20 when my legs started to spasm and I was reduced to a shuffle. With an illustrious medical history that included watching *ER* and *Casualty*, I concluded that a good stretch would sort it all out. Stopping on the grass verge by the side of the course, I did some stretching, but whatever I did wasn't helpful as the spasms only worsened, running from toe to shoulder with my legs seemingly locked.

Screaming and on the point of tears, I reassured a concerned passing runner that I didn't need emergency services assistance, resolved to leave medical diagnosis to the experts and to walk/hobble the rest of the way in. With four miles to go I felt comparatively better. The various ailments amounted to a general, all-over feeling of exhaustion and pain which was somehow easier to deal with.

Almost enjoying the next mile I overheard two

runners wondering if they'd make the five-hour cut-off and whether we'd be given a medal anyway. With that I calculated, at current pace, I wasn't going to make it. My time goals had all been missed, and the final one of just finishing was looking less than likely. I'd never even seriously considered the cut-off time when I entered. I adopted my now trademark finish of grinding out the last few miles in a horrendous slumped forward angle, head lolling to one side, eyes fixed on the ground, arms pumping pathetically sideways like Peter Kay en route to Amarillo.

Unbeknown to me, my top had chafed so much across my shoulders I'd rubbed a mole clean off and a large worrying blood stain was forming across my back, giving me a Julius Caesar appearance, except this stab wound was self-inflicted. One of the final marshals was highly concerned about my general state of health, which I found comforting if not a little mystifying. 'Who's bleeding? Me? Am I?'

In the final section my brain became completely fuddled and, although I had passed the finish line on each of the previous laps, I struggled to recall how much further I had to run. Was it to before the tower blocks or just after? If before, I'd finish before the cut-off. If after, I was likely to be ranked Disqualified (DQ) or Did Not Finish (DNF). What would happen after five hours? Do they pack up and go home? Do they erect a barrier to prevent stragglers crossing the line? Would the last five horrible, horrible hours be for nothing? Why do people do this? It's an awful way to spend your weekend when pubs and beer exist.

Rounding a corner, I entered the sort of alleyway normally seen on TV, bedecked in police crime tape, with the finish line ahead in the centre of the estate. Cloë was waiting, with our son and a worried facial expression. Realising I must look as bad as I felt, I broke into what I like to think was a glorious sprint finish. More likely I resembled a man falling downstairs without the aid of stairs. I crossed the line, broken, in 4h57m. I wasn't quite the last to finish, but felt like it as no other runners were around.

The volunteer handing out medals had to be stirred from her standing nap to present me with my medal and a commemorative Luton Marathon facecloth, the first of many odd commemorative goodies received over the years. The marathon had all but finished me.

My target times now looked laughable. The delusion of reeling in other runners in the second half was embarrassing. Had I gone much slower, I would have been the one being reeled in by the tail runners. After giving Cloë a sweaty, tear-stained cuddle we went to collect our daughter and go home.

Against all logic though, and despite barely being able to run at the start of the year, I was now a marathon runner. I felt different. Somehow a better person. Yet somehow not quite 'done'.

While any sensible person would have run one marathon and stopped, I didn't. Stubbornness runs in my family, unlike running. I'd been overtaken at around mile 20 by what, in my rush of youth, I would call a very elderly gentleman. The octogenarian was dressed as Superman, sauntering along at what seemed an effortless pace. We briefly chatted (OK, I wheezed) about his running. It was a fateful few minutes as I learnt of the existence of the 100 Marathon Club and, in the back of my mind, a decision was made that I would try to join them.

You make funny decisions when your brain lacks oxygen.

Training for your first marathon

Main advice: join a club. The improvements you will make in fitness and performance will startle you, not to mention the improved safety of running in groups is hard to beat. Which club you join will depend as much on your location and what days fit with your schedule as anything else. In Milton Keynes I was spoilt for choice. Most clubs had two or more midweek runs and one long run on the weekend. Some preferred Saturday, others Sunday, so I could take my pick considering kids' clubs or other family commitments.

It's often said that even a non-runner can complete a marathon after three or four months of training, but the better your base level of fitness the more comfortable you'll be. Most training programmes are 16–18 weeks and tailored for varying levels of experience. Although marathons are run every weekend throughout the year, there tends to be a big push for spring due to London Marathon being 'THE' marathon (Brighton, Manchester, Milton Keynes are also BIG though due to a course measurement issue, Manchester was the shortest marathon as well for three years!), and a slightly smaller push for an autumn marathon (Bournemouth, Abingdon, Chester, York). These fit the traditional approach of one or two marathons a year, rather than the one or two a weekend that some of the more hard-core runners aim for.

The advantage of targeting a spring event is that most clubs tailor their training schedules towards them, as do all of the running magazines. It also coincides with New Year resolutions to get fit. The start of the year is a wake-up call to all those who got a London Marathon place in the October ballot but have yet to get out the front door and make a start.

Most training plans will incorporate several races, often a half marathon and then a 20-mile race, usually run in early spring. They are a good measure of progress and also provide experience of the whole process of big scale races. You can turn up to parkrun moments before the start, throw your hoodie in a bush for later and set off. For big events the process of storing kit, collecting numbers and toilet queues can take hours and be daunting to first-timers.

For this reason, I'd recommend tackling one of the larger half marathons in the lead-up. Silverstone and Reading are popular for those in the south of the UK. Neither is particularly scenic but both afford the size and feel of big marathon events.

Where possible, try and pick a half marathon with a similar course and elevation gain (how much uphill you go) as your intended marathon. If you live in Norfolk, do all runs on the broads, and have never run up or down a hill, you're going to struggle on race day on Mount Snowdon.

The marathon training schedules can appear daunting, probably appearing before you as a colour-coded table with apparently random numbers and acronyms covering every square. The few sections you do initially understand can be scary and off-putting. 'In three weeks I've got to run how far...?' Every journey begins with a single step so just relax and take each day as it comes.

The goal of any programme is to get you to the starting line fit and able to complete the course. Irrespective of whether the aim is simply to get around the course, or to set a PB and qualify for future races, the approach will be largely the same. Each week will have faster-paced sessions to increase speed, and a long run at the weekend to increase distance and endurance and prepare your legs to carry you to the finish. Some might include hill sessions or very short intervals at faster pace. Most programmes have a minimum of three runs per week; more advanced will have many more and even two sessions on single days.

It's common for programmes to build the run distance gradually, then step back down for a week to allow legs to recover before cranking back up again. If it's your first event you may only hit 20 miles once in training, or may be limited to a three- or four-hour run with no distance goal. The reasoning behind stopping at 20 is that the further six miles of training would take a toll on your legs requiring recovery that would hinder further training and offer no real benefit. Accepting this can be hard, knowing that the 'little bit extra' you'll need to run on race day was considered an impressive run on fresh legs several months ago. Trust the programme and trust the experience of thousands of people who have followed the same path.

A key part of the training is making sure you're running at the correct pace relative to your expected marathon pace (MP). For experienced runners this is easier. Novices may not even have a pace in mind. In this case, there are several online calculators that will estimate race times based on distances already run. They are not infallible but give a good starting point.

Typically, your marathon pace (with sufficient training) will be 8–10 per cent slower than your half marathon pace, which is itself 8–10 per cent slower than your 10k pace.

Once you have a target pace in mind, the sessions will likely be run at steady pace (one minute slower than MP), easy/comfortable (able to talk while running), or fast interval work at a pace you believe you can maintain. Sections of marathon pace are often included, especially on the long run, to get you used to running on tired legs. Don't be disheartened in the early weeks. It's a long schedule and improvements will come.

The one looming spectre of defeat in a training period is the prospect of injury but, assuming you follow the gradual progression of the plan, you should keep it at bay. If you miss a session don't try and make it up the next day as you will end up tired and underperforming.

Other steps to avoid injury are to cross-train,

otherwise known as 'some other sort of exercise': swimming, weights, rowing machine, cross trainer, cycling or whatever takes your fancy. Keep active, improve fitness and avoid excessive impact from running.

If injury does hit, stay calm. Don't fight through like a 'trooper' as you'll likely aggravate it. Better to stop and rest and return fit. A runner can miss a cumulative two weeks of a marathon training plan with negligible effects.

The key runs are the long ones. If you miss these, arrange to run others.

Focusing on the long runs for your first marathon

It's not uncommon to feel awful on your final long training runs. Marathon pace will feel hard as you're banking serious mileage. You may even be hit by doubts about your ability to run the distance. Twenty miles felt hard, how are you going to manage a further six? Try not to stress. The programmes are proven, and countless other runners have had those doubts. As intensity reduces in the final few weeks the body recovers, and you are likely to approach the main event like a coiled spring. Even then, the crowds and other runners will drag you through the final few miles.

The key part of training is not just to build fitness but also to test everything. Your debut event should be 'merely' a matter of running a little further than before, hopefully at a slightly faster pace. Your morning routine, pre-race preparation, running kit and fuelling are now all known and proven. There should be no surprises on the big day.

As your long runs lengthen, you're going to need to start taking on extra fuel, and it's worth checking what will be available on race day. Most big events give out energy gels and sports drinks. If you can determine what brand they are you'll be able to take them in training to ensure they work for you. You don't want to find out at mile 18 of your debut marathon that the provided gels cause you to re-engage with your breakfast.

Gels are very marmite. Some runners can down gel after gel while others only get on well with certain brands. Some won't be able to stomach them in any form and find them as appealing as a shot of tequila, and even more likely to result in being sick. Sports drinks tend to be less of an issue but are still worth checking.

In one of your final long runs you should wear the exact running kit you intend to use on the day. From trainers to hats and socks to sunglasses, it should all be tested. Better to discover now that your sports bra rubs like hell when you sweat, and work out how to avoid it. Once tested it can all be washed and put away for the race. It's worth remembering that if you're targeting a spring marathon, it will probably be a lot warmer than your training runs. Long daybreak runs on frosty March mornings were completed in single digit temperatures, far lower than you're going to experience in London on a warm April Sunday. Don't be the guy who spends most of the race casting off clothes like a travelling burlesque show. You won't win a friend when your sweat-soaked top smacks a passing runner in the face.

Elaborate fancy dress will also need a trial run, concentrating on where it rubs, visibility, and how you plan to drink and eat during the race. Encased in suit and prosthetic head you're going to sweat heavily while struggling to drink without at least a straw.

Morning routine is the polite reference to making sure your body has done the necessary emptying before you hit the start. During training you'll have learnt what it takes from waking up and how long before your digestion gets going. A good strong cup of coffee helps get most things moving. Try a few different breakfasts to see what works for you, with a view to what's going to be available on the day. If you're staying in a budget hotel you're unlikely to manage a free-range egg white omelette with fresh avocado, Sicilian pine nuts and wild mushrooms, but will have to make do with unbranded cereal and suspicious sausages. Typical preferences are bananas, porridge and cereal. Personally, I find the blend of fat, protein, carbs and stodge in a cooked breakfast works well.

The Last Few Weeks of Marathon Training

Most marathon training programmes last between 12 and 18 weeks with tapering starting two to three weeks out. Tapering is where the volume of training starts to reduce, with the intention of entering the race with fresh legs and bursting with energy. Final long runs are typically three hours at three weeks out, 2h–2h30m at two weeks out and 1h–1h30m one week out. Since you are now as fit as you're going to be, this is an opportunity to plan and assess.

Should my knee make that odd noise? Be mindful of any niggles or injuries and bear them in mind on any further runs. It's better to approach the race fit and a little undertrained than well trained but injured. Don't cram in extra sessions to make up for missed runs. There's little improvement you can make in the last two to three weeks but a whole lot of damage you might do if you behave like a fool.

Feeling Hot, Hot, Hot? It's worth trying to get a run in at similar time of day as your marathon. Brighton Marathon had heat issues in 2017 (apparently not helped by poor decisions on water stations). Having doubtless trained for months on frosty early mornings the marathoners struggled when attempting the same pace at midday. Bag some weekend leave from the family and try an hour or so in the sun. Better to realise now that you need a peaked cap to keep the sun off your bald head than when you wake up in the medical tent with sunstroke.

Drinking for beginners: let's think about hydration. First, check race instructions. Many events now use cups to save waste, rather than bottles, and some people get on great with these. Personally, I get barely a dribble down, along with a lot of air which leads to choking and a spontaneous regurgitation of the last gel. Adoring family members who have waited on a grass verge for two hours only to see you vomit down the back of the runner in front now have to pretend they don't know you.

Experiment with cups (just running around the garden if necessary). Pinching the cup can help, or slowing down to a walk. If neither works, try a hand bottle or even a rucksack with a bladder (Camelbak or similar) and take your own water. Another cheap option is Powerade sports drink, which comes in a sports bottle with a wide opening which can be filled from cups as you go. At the end of the race you can bin it before your Paula Radcliffe sprint to glory.

My toes poke out my shoes, do I need new ones? Time now to check your trainers. If you've used one pair for the whole training programme they may be past their best. If they are beyond help you have time to buy a replacement (same style, same make, same size, nothing different) and break them in before race day.

Get your kit off (and laid on the bed). Include everything you intend to wear, carry or use. Do you suddenly realise that the gels you intend to use have nowhere to go, or your phone doesn't fit in your shorts pocket? Or maybe your club top clashes with your socks and you'll never live it down. Address these issues now.

Pin the bib on your top, attach the timing chip to your shoes and visually check you have everything. Now, if you wake up late, you won't panic and wonder where your left shoe is. Of course in the age of social media it is pretty much compulsory to take a photo of the 'flat lay' on the spare bed and post it for others to encourage/ criticise poor choice of top e.g. 'You're not going to wear that, are you?' Try not to be misled by others to make sudden changes.

I can('t) hear music? Check final race instructions. An increasing number of races ban headphones for safety reasons, and will either remove you from the results or even remove you from the course. Some will allow use of bone conductor units, which don't go in the ear so don't block out traffic noise and marshals' instructions. If you absolutely must have music for your legs to function you still have time to buy some.

People struggle to understand how seasons work. Check the long-range weather forecast, adjust what you're wearing, and plan for discarding clothes. I've lost track of how many spring events I've stood next to a guy decked head to toe in black full-length compression wear, knowing they'll regret it in a few miles and need to do a quick striptease in a portaloo, or run into a post while tangled in their top. If you're not going to be cold standing in just your running gear you are wearing too much and you will suffer later in the race.

Even the most streamlined marathon will leave you waiting half an hour after getting rid of your drop bag. You need layers you can lose at the start and not carry around the course. Tripping over the expensive jumper tied around your waist is not good. Have an old tee shirt/jumper or bin liner ready to dispose of at the start. Most marathons collect discarded clothes for charity.

How are you getting there? Plan your travel. Roads will likely be busy (Manchester Marathon in 2016 managed a brilliant own goal of closing the roads to the event parking), and trains may be running reduced services. Where do you plan to park and how long a walk is it to the start? Working back from entering the start pen, how long do you need to drop bags and queue for toilets? Allow extra time for crowds and other issues. For a big event, arriving two hours before the start is not excessive. Allow more if picking up a race pack on the day. You can be surprised by how early you need to get up, and might find you'd be better booking a nearby hotel.

Drop Bag: think about what you want in your drop bag, or for your other half to hold. Few marathons will have showers or changing rooms. The logistics of getting 10,000 runners washed are formidable. A fresh set of clothes can, therefore, be a lifesaver.

Last-minute items for use before dropping off bag:

- Sun cream. It's fine, I hear you claim, I never burn in the UK when spending 12 hours a day in an office. Why would I burn over seven hours outdoors, barely dressed and in direct sun?
- Bin bag/disposable clothes
- Vaseline and plasters for final application
- Last-minute food or drink
- Sandwich bag for iPod/phone if the weather looks hot

or rainy (it's an expensive event if your new iPhone gets soaked)

For use after the race:
- Wet wipes to freshen up
- Underwear and clothes (don't forget socks and a welcoming hoodie)
- Fresh shoes or flip-flops
- Plasters
- Carrier bag for your stinky gear
- Any post-race food or drink
- Emergency foil blanket (most races give these out. If you decline you might find much later on the bus home you're in need of one)
- Directions or location of agreed meet-up point with family and friends (you're tired and can't remember if you're meeting in the Three Kings or Kings Head pub)
- Power pack for phone (you've flattened phone playing power ballads for five hours. Now you can't ring your hubby or post that vital selfie to Facebook)
- Cash or credit card for essential post-race beer

It may sound excessive, planning all this ahead, but pre-race nerves will hit soon. The more prepared you are the better.

Final marathon advice for first-timers

In over 100 marathons I've made every mistake possible. So, distilled below is my 'wisdom' so you don't have to make the mistakes.

Stick to the plan.

You've tested your breakfast, your snacks.

You've tested your pre-race poop strategy.

You've tested what you're going to run in.

You've tested what fuel and hydration you'll take on during your run.

You've tested sunglasses, hat or headband.

If you have long hair like me (cough cough), you've tested what combination of plaits/bunches/ponytail/dreadlocks/Mohawk works best for you.

You've planned what to leave in your drop bag for after the race (warm hoodie, wet wipes, dry clothes).

You've planned what to wear while waiting in your start pen (bin bags are a good look).

You've decided what pace you're going to run and tested it in training.

GO IN YOUR KIT

It's all been laid out ready as before. Wear extra layers on top but ideally the first items you put on will be your complete running kit.

Travelling several hours from home to realise you're still wearing the flip-flops you wear to put the bins out is not ideal.

ARRIVE EARLY

Allow time for several things to go wrong. Hopefully

they won't, and you can sit under a tree, relax and soak up the atmosphere. If they do go wrong you've got time to spare.

Allow for travelling to the venue through busy traffic and park/walk from bus/lock up bike. Everything will take longer than you expect.

Join a toilet queue. Double-check you have everything, and queue to drop off your bag. Toilet queue again. Warm up muscles. Join the crowd for the start pens. Realise you need another wee. Join the toilet queue again. Rejoin pen, etc. Set off.

THINGS CAN GO WRONG
Trains run late, cars break down. Parking and traffic management take time. After training for months, with countless hours spent pounding away, you don't want to blow it for an extra 30 minutes of beauty sleep. No amount of extra time in bed will improve the finishing photos.

AVOID GOAL CREEP
You've planned and practised a pace. Your taper has worked, and you feel great. Don't be tempted to increase the pace. If you get to mile 20 and feel good, push then, NOT at mile three. Every minute too fast on the first half will cost you two on the second. Get tricked into aiming for a 4h45m rather than your planned five-hour and you'll likely blow up and miss the five-hour.

STICK TO THE PLAN – BUT ALSO ADAPT!
If something goes wrong don't panic.

You reach down for your final gel to realise it's fallen out. Hope is not lost! Swig an energy drink and power on.

Your GPS watch or Garmin goes flat. You have no idea what pace you're doing. Rely on mile markers and ask other runners, run on feel. If it feels too fast slow down.

The gel makes you gag and threaten to vomit. Stop taking them. Stomach cramps and hair matted with sick will slow you more than a marginal loss in fuel.

You didn't see a loved one at mile 12 and now you're miserable. They're probably stuck in crowds, or maybe they saw you but you missed them. Keep going.

It's way hotter than your practice runs. Tip water over your head, bin some clothes, roll up sleeves, run in shade when able and slow down. London Marathon in 2018 was the hottest on record. Those that finished well slowed to account. Those that walked it in reminiscent of an extra from a zombie film did not.

Most importantly though: enjoy!

This is your first marathon. Less than 1 per cent of the population have run a marathon so you're joining an exclusive club. Whether you glide over the line in a world record time or drag yourself across like a drunken student, you have achieved the distance and earned the medal.

First marathon done? Let's confess.

The marathon has been and gone. You've run out of people to impress with your awesome medal and amazing tales of needing help getting off the office loo when your legs locked up.

Now it's all done we can be grown-ups and admit the secret truth… Stop here if still training for your first marathon. Do not read down! OK, THEN ?

FACT: Marathon running is amazing but training for it sucks. Really sucks. It's probably the worst thing you'll ever put yourself through voluntarily. Possibly childbirth is worse but I can't make a meaningful comparison.

- Muscles you didn't even know you had have ached to the point of interrupting your sleep.

- You ceased to have a right and left leg, they're now simply the 'good one' and the 'bad one'.

- You've chafed in places you'd rather never have to touch.

- If you have a committed training partner you may even have applied lube to another person. In broad daylight. In public. Sicko.

- Public nudity is now 'fine' when stripping off manky running gear in a deserted car park because you're in a large group all doing the same. Yes, the same justification people use when arrested for dogging.

- You've run when you couldn't feel your fingers and when you wish you couldn't feel your dodgy ankle.

- If your bowels haven't cooperated you've probably done things in the woods a bear would blush at. Sometimes you may not have even made it to the woods in time. Or even managed to pull your shorts down.

- Sharting. Never trust a fart after mile 18.

- You've learnt your body is a veritable factory of gross stuff as sweat, snot, phlegm, vomit, tears and blood all compete to leave it by any available means.

- Falling, tripping, running into things and clipping your shoulder are somehow normal. Any run finished without gaining a bruise or graze is noteworthy.

- The reward for a long run is a longer run. 12 miles today? See you next week for 14, try not to dwell on how you rang your husband at mile nine advising him to find someone else and move on if you never make it back alive.

- Tiredness has become a normal state. Any movie trip or theatre show is now interrupted by an hour of all-consuming unconsciousness and you need to try and piece the plot back together upon awakening.

- The constant hunger. You got anything I can eat? A ketchup sachet from the glovebox is a suitable replacement for the gel you forgot to pack. Right?

- Morning winter runs have proven it's possible for sweat to freeze on contact with the air.

- You've needed assistance to remove headwear frozen to your scalp.

- You now accept that getting out of bed is something done in slow stages like the evolution of man from ape. The progression is re-enacted as you crawl from the duvet to finally stand triumphant under the shower, pondering if you're getting ready for work or a run or maybe only got up for a wee after all.

- You've missed nights down the pub or come back early as you needed to join other idiots at stupid o'clock in the morning to go for a run of such length it could prove fatal.

If anyone had told you how rubbish it would be when you started, the only marathon you'd have contemplated would be on Netflix, but shhhh! You're now part of the group so it's your duty to keep this quiet.

Much like childbirth you need to focus on the outcome and not dismay prospective runners with the truth. Running a marathon is amazing and everyone should do it, but on no account should they be warned how bad the training will be.

Work colleagues may approach the new athletic version of you, amazed at your achievement and ask for marathon advice. Do you give them the full horror? No. You smile, tell them it's hard but rewarding, and advise them to 'go for it'. You cruel, misleading fork-tongued marathoner! They're probably within their rights to come find you afterwards and punch you in the mouth. They won't of course, as they'll be too busy showing you their medal and regaling you with their mile splits.

There's more. Here's the next secret: maintaining fitness is easier than getting there.

A couple of runs a week can be enough to keep you ticking over. Take advantage of the upside. You can chase the kids in the garden without passing out in the shrubbery. Five-a-side football matches with your mates don't leave you dry heaving into the kit bag. When you run to the door for the postman you not only make it before the 'sorry you're out' slip hits the mat but open the door looking human, not sweat-drenched and red-faced like you've been interrupted midway through something embarrassing.

You said just one...

The other reason you may want to maintain your fitness is for the next marathon. You were only going to run one, but you've got a PB now so you might as well try and beat it. Did I mention there's a club for people who have run 100 marathons? Wouldn't that be good?

ACT 2

IF SOMETHING HURTS, KEEP DOING IT

5

26.2 MILES AGAIN

Marathon 2 – London

Late in 2011 I managed to secure a charity spot for the London Marathon, running for Cystic Fibrosis (my employer's chosen charity). My initial excitement at running THE marathon in 2012, the London Olympic year, was dampened by the requirement to raise £2,000. Deciding that more was better, and suffering through two events would likely raise more than just one, I also signed up for the inaugural Milton Keynes Marathon which was due to take place a week later. Having barely completed one marathon, attempting to undertake two in a week was idiotic enough to attract some hard-earned cash from friends and colleagues.

Realising the need to actually train for the marathon this time, I started following MK Marathon on social media. Having missed a spot on one of their organised training runs around the area, I inquired on Facebook if more were planned. As luck would have it Chris, a local runner and coach with MK Lakeside Runners, saw my post and invited me along. Although I'd previously considered joining a club I'd soon thrown the idea in the 'nope' bucket along with learning to play the guitar, swim the channel and eat properly. Running clubs are full of runners and, as we all know, runners are weird. They wear odd mismatched sportswear, fancy watches and head torches, and converse loudly about splits and PBs.

At this stage I didn't consider myself to be a runner, just a bloke that ran a bit. I also have a near pathological hatred of meeting new people. Despite all this I did something as out of character as that first run almost 12 months previously. I went along in the dark to find a group of strangers, introduce myself and run with them. The sort of thing a real runner would do. Shudder.

I enjoyed my first few sessions. Everyone introduced themselves and was friendly, but I promptly forgot all their names and still call the less regular members 'mate' to avoid having to ask their names again. This after six years of running together.

Running with a club provides training and motivation. With set goals and targeted races, you can't just run aimlessly on your own and hope you magically get better. Instead you need a structured training plan, with key runs designed to build your performance and gradually increase the miles. Knowing there is a group of like-minded idiots meeting by a windswept lake on a cold winter's evening gives the extra push needed to get out and join them.

I became a member of MK Lakeside Runners and

gradually improved. In hindsight, I wish I had joined the previous year.

There are two main clubs in Milton Keynes for recreational runners, MK Lakeside and Redway Runners. More by luck than judgement, I'd joined the one that didn't have lurid green running tops. There's a friendly rivalry between the two and Cloë's decision to join Redway Runners a few years later has prompted more than a few Romeo and Juliet jokes when we pose for pre-race photos in rival kit.

Most UK clubs have various groups at differing abilities from 'I think I'd like to run' through to 'I reckon I could take Mo in a fair race'. To find your local one check online (EA Athletics is a good start, but the home page of your local parkrun website will list them) or strike up a conversation with a club-top-wearing runner. Typically, the club will let you try a few sessions free, and most have structured training from Couch to 5k, to marathon and beyond. The comradeship is a great booster at local races where fellow club members and their families will cheer you on whether you're leading the pack or dragging your sweaty and bloodstained club top to a dead f*cking last (DFL) finish.

For the bargain hunters, clubs typically organise discounts to local races and being a member of an England Athletics affiliated club will get you a few quid off most entry fees, not to mention discount at many running shops. Membership costs vary from £5 but are mostly £20–£30 per year, with membership of England Athletics as an additional cost if required.

If a recent parent, you may be able to find local buggy

running groups where you can combine training and socialising while getting the baby some fresh air and working up an appetite for a post-run cake and coffee.

On my first long Saturday club run there was frost on the ground and an outside temperature of −12°C, almost unheard of in Milton Keynes. I turned up wearing pretty much every item of technical running gear I had to prove to them and myself that I was serious about training, but also practising my disappointed face for when it was inevitably cancelled.

It wasn't. They complained about the cold, paused to mock poor Stephen for turning up in shorts and short sleeves, and we were off. That day I learnt never to underestimate the stupidity of a large group of runners and also that sweat in your hat can freeze into a solid lump.

For the next three months my weekends changed from fast parkrun efforts to longer, slower runs as the mileage grew. Despite having run a marathon I found the initial long runs of around ten miles hard work, coming after two structured sessions in the week. Tuesday night was typically a technical run with hill repeats or short intervals, while Thursday was a longer run with sections at marathon or half marathon pace. I remember my legs being heavy and aching for much of the time, but I got used to it over the following year and it became almost a point of honour.

While the coaches battled with my poor running form, my overall pace and endurance improved greatly. They began to suggest that, with further training and favourable conditions, not only could I beat my optimistic 4h30m marathon target, but that a sub 4h might be possible. In March I entered the local MK Half Marathon and, despite atrocious weather and a sneaky hill in the last mile, managed a 1h42m half, more than ten minutes improvement on my previous best. The weekly mileage continued to increase, and meeting the club at crack of Saturday's dawn became the norm.

These runs were not easy, and the later stages were ground out behind grimaced faces while the coaches and more experienced runners did their best to motivate us. 'These are the miles that will really count on race day, you'll be thankful you did these!'

'Good, because right now I'm contemplating falling in the canal just to make it stop.'

I'd drag myself home afterwards tired and sore, but pleased to have done a long run before most people were out of bed.

The first few attempts at 20 mile runs were real milestones. Although sometimes it felt more like I'd run with a millstone. On my final 20 miler I managed to break three hours (by seconds). The same distance in the Luton Marathon four months previously had taken me almost four hours, so I could start to believe a sub four-hour marathon was possible. I'd have an hour to cover the remaining 6.2 miles.

Silverstone Half Marathon

As final preparation for London I looked around for a big half marathon to get me ready. The options locally were Reading or Silverstone raceway. With my interest in motorsport, I chose the latter. What could be better than running around the actual track Hamilton and Senna have hammered?

As it turns out, almost anything.

Knowing Silverstone has traffic issues I allowed plenty of time to park and walk to the start area. The Run To The Beat Half had shown just how long everything can take. I dropped off my bag, made the toilet ritual and assembled in the start pen. With a tendency towards too many events, I'd run the local MK half the previous weekend in bitterly cold conditions of hail and snow. I'd finished sodden and cold, and glad of the emergency blankets issued at the end. This being typically temperamental British spring weather, seven days later the sky was clear, there was not a breeze and, at 10am, the sun was strong. Temperatures were predicted to hit 14°C, an oven compared to the previous event. Many people were using the last few minutes to shed layers.

We waited for the start, and waited some more. Traffic chaos on the site meant a sizeable number of runners were still trying to park so the start was delayed. Men hurdled the Armco and used the wait as a good excuse to water the grass around the tyre bales. Women wished they could do likewise.

Eventually we set off around the hallowed track of Silverstone. The smooth wide track was great to run. It was wide: really, really wide. Without cutting through the pack I found myself alternating between the inside of the bend and the far outside, therefore covering additional distance. It is almost impossible to run only 13.1 miles unless you're at the front or back of the pack.

The other issue with Silverstone is how exposed the track is, with just gravel traps and wide expanses of grass on either side. This is great for watching the F1 heroes, rubbish for sheltering runners. We got baked; in other years, runners were lashed and blown by the full brunt of the British spring.

Running around the F1 track is brilliant for 100 metres and for a brief section through the pit lanes. For the rest of the time it's basically deserted and about as interesting as cutting through a supermarket car park. Even parkruns get more spectators and support than Silverstone HM so it's hard to maintain motivation.

Enthusiasm waning, I finished slower than for my rain sodden, hilly attempt the previous week. The event is worth doing once as experience of a big event...but only once.

Marathon No 2 – London Marathon Weekend 2012

Small events either post you the bib, or you collect it on the morning of the race from a chap hunched over an old pasting table. Big events go one better and hold a bizarre combination of market stall and trade fair known as an Expo for you to collect your bib. For London I chose to go to the Expo on the Saturday.

Nervous and excited, I checked I had my confirmation letter and photo ID, several dozen times, before getting dropped at the tube by the family. Trekking across London to the Excel Exhibition Centre made me wonder why they would choose to hold the Expo in such an awkward location. I now realise that all marathon Expos take place in slightly run-down halls in the dingiest parts of the city. It could be a plot by the marathon organisers to make sure you see the worst bits, and therefore appreciate the picturesque course so much more. Or it could be because the halls are cheap.

After collecting my number and suffering several hours looking at stalls selling unnecessary supplements and gear, I returned to Kilburn and my family. We were to stay with Cloë's aunt in North London that night as the earliest train from Milton Keynes didn't arrive in time for the start. After a pasta dinner I went to bed wondering if this second attempt, one I'd actually trained for, might be less awful than Luton.

In the morning I tiptoed around the room as quietly as possible, dressing in my club vest (like a proper runner), adding several old tee shirts and a woolly hat that I planned to discard at the start. Sneaking out of the house, I walked to Woodside station to find that trains on a Sunday were less regular than I expected. On the platform I was joined by another runner with kit bag slung over his shoulder, wearing an assortment of ripped and dishevelled throwaway clothes.

On the train into London I began to regret staying over the night before, as we seemed to stop at every station, but after switching trains for Maze Hill things changed. We gathered runners at every stop. In fact, we were herded into the train like cattle going to market.

Other entrants warn you about the scale of major marathon starts, but you can't really appreciate it without experiencing it. The park was a sea of people:

joining queues, dropping bags, stretching or trying to snag yet another free sports drink from the stands. Inexperienced though I was, I could still see that downing three bottles of Lucozade an hour before the race would lead to multiple portaloo stops.

If you're lucky enough to get a place for London, be sure to soak it all in. Nothing else is like it for mass hysteria and nerves mixed with excitement and foreboding. The fancy dress runners are a key part of the experience, and spotting cartoon or movie characters is as much a thrill for other runners as the spectators. My favourite was a group of four men in Lycra body suits and crash helmets who were unappealing, and not very memorable, until they stood in formation and lifted a beautifully crafted bobsled to become the Jamaican team that competed at the 1988 Winter Olympics team and were the basis of *Cool Runnings*, a classic from my youth.

The excitement was contagious. It was a beautiful, clear spring morning, and I was actually going to run London!

Even as a kid growing up I had been dimly aware of the event and the superhuman men and women who undertook it. Now I was going to be one. I dropped my bag in the lorries, made a few more toilet trips (you never know) and went to the start pen.

I was in Red 5, with the more ponderous and painful fancy dress runners consigned to Red 9. In the pen I chatted to other runners and listened to conversations. This was the first time I'd heard negativity and worry on such a scale. I've come to appreciate that much of this is sandbagging to get your excuses for a poor performance in early and save face in front of your clubmates and other runners: Bob did rubbish today but he explained how a wild bear ripped his leg off the day before and had to be re-attached with duct tape so finish time was OK considering.

At the time it seemed every conversation was describing an injury that nearly kept them at home, explaining in detail how much training they hadn't done, or bemoaning the hot weather, wrong choice of shoes or poor sleep in a dodgy B&B around the corner. There wasn't a single voice extolling the virtues of their training runs, confident in their abilities to tackle this herculean task.

Almost everyone had doubts and fears: about finishing the event, being at the agreed point to wave at your partner, or securing a qualification time for Boston. Whatever your doubts, the final minutes before the event are not the time to dwell on them. Think happy thoughts and, if the runner next to you is regaling you with how he finished his last event on a stretcher, explain you need to meet a fictitious friend on the other side of the pen and move away. You don't need negativity. Instead, reflect on how well training has gone, or when you smashed the pace and kept up with a faster club mate.

We began just after 10am, hot on the heels of the elites and 'good for age' runners. I wasn't sure how long it would take me to cross the start line. I'd worked out my splits for a four-hour marathon, had them taped on my wrist and given a copy to Cloë, letting her know I could be anything up to 15 minutes late due to the start.

In reality, it took only five minutes. Against all logic and reason, the fat kid from school was going to run London.

Starts are organised well, so you're not held up too much, but sheer numbers means you could probably lift your feet and be carried along by the crush. After two miles as much on pace as congestion allowed, I settled into a rhythm, keeping as close to 8:45minute/miles as I could, even though it felt very easy. This would give a finish time of around 3h55m depending on what distance I ended up running.

I tried to follow the blue painted line on the course for the shortest route, but the dense crowd meant it wasn't always possible. I resolved not to stress and to enjoy the relatively relaxed run in a beautiful city, shedding a tear crossing Tower Bridge at mile 12, a real high point. The crowds are among the deepest, and the wall of noise is amazing.

Another tip: if you wear sunglasses at London, no one can see how much you cry like a big baby.

For almost the whole route the crowd is three or four deep. Great for the runners, but it makes moving around the course almost impossible for spectators. I missed Cloë on many of the scheduled stops as she got stuck on the tube. Some stations were closed to avoid crushing. At least once I ran straight past, oblivious to her cheers.

At halfway I was on target and feeling good, but my GPS watch was beeping for the miles a long way before the marker posts. Either it was over-reading or I was running very wide. Deciding to ignore the watch pace, I concentrated on the mile markers and elapsed time on my watch only. It seemed to work well, and I crossed off miles as planned.

For nutrition I used the gels I'd used in training, although they were sickly sweet and took some swallowing. As the race wore on they became harder to stomach and I increased the gaps from the recommended 20 minutes to 30–40 to avoid the taste.

At 20 miles I felt sure that my pace was good and I suffered none of the issues encountered at Luton. The pebble on the beach analogy came true and I passed runner after runner. I'd kept to my pace, so I reckon they must have set off faster and were now paying the price. With a pleasing feeling of perfect pacing (seldom encountered on future races) I started to push to ensure I would finish well under four hours. Cloë and her brother were leaning over the barrier at the Houses of Parliament right turn. They cheered and bellowed and, thanks to them, I found new reserves of energy, picking my way through the field ever more quickly, dodging around the cramp-stricken, stumbling wrecks that I remembered all too well from Luton.

Rounding the final, Buckingham Palace, corner I could believe that it was going to happen. Despite recording a distance of 26.8 miles on my watch, the increased pace had been enough. I crossed the line in 3h54m, well under my four-hour target with over an hour off my previous time five months earlier.

London Marathon, like a lot of big events, has regular chip timing mats, used to generate statistics and produce charts and graphs for the statistically obsessed. I pushed the final 5k through a sea of slower runners, passing, the tracking system later told me, over 5,000 runners and being overtaken by a mere handful. I'd also managed a negative split, with the second half marginally quicker than the first. Considered by many to be the mark of a perfectly paced race, it stops you blowing up in the final stages. If every race went like this marathon running would be the most rewarding pursuit going.

After collecting my goody bag and extended family, we attended the post-race party and enjoyed food, celebratory hugs and a leg massage. I was on a complete runner's high and looking forward to recounting the race with my club mates the following week.

London Marathon had been everything it's meant to be, and for once I'd done everything a runner is meant to do.

London Marathon Course Notes

Getting to the start line is no small feat. I'm not referring to the months of training and injury avoidance, but to the actual travel. There are three start zones for the event. The blue start at Blackheath is a mixture of championship places (the very fast) and ballot runners. Green start is also from Blackheath and has a lot of the celebrities as well as the faster world record attempts (fastest superhero, etc). Red start at Greenwich Park is for charity runners and often has the fancy dress costumes, but with some of the fast 'good for age' at the front in a separate pen.

Green and blue meet after a mile, while red doesn't

join until after mile three. Both routes are measured to be the correct length, but the split course means that runners thin out before they meet. If you're desperate to see a friend from another start, it's worth arranging somewhere to meet along the course.

London Marathon appoint pacers to help you achieve your best: seasoned runners well within their abilities. Spread throughout the start pens, they typically range from 3h to 5h15m. All will run at a steady pace a few seconds under the target pace, excepting the 5h15m pacers who may be using a run, walk approach. You'll be able to identify them by the large flags attached to them with start zone and finish time. Don't be alarmed to see them out of order on the course. It's entirely possible the red 3h30m pacer started ahead of the blue 3h15m pacer, so will be ahead of them for a good chunk of the marathon.

The first six miles can go from exciting ('Hey, look, there's the cameras!') to a little disappointing ('There's people everywhere, I can't even see the road') but the chanting and yelling when the two groups join at mile three is a good experience and, at mile six, you loop around the Cutty Sark ship, an iconic moment for any runner.

After the high point of Tower Bridge follows a long section approaching the Docklands area where you will see the faster runners, possibly even the leaders, heading back on the other side nearly ten miles ahead of you. It's there, every year, that a few cheaters jump the barrier to get a better time. Even some 'celebs' (using the term loosely to describe former girl/boyfriends of reality TV stars) have fallen foul of the media as a result of trying to shave some distance off.

Fast-forward several miles and you'll be the other side of the barriers at mile 23 with just a simple run along the Embankment to finish the race. The crowds will be deep, and many of the charities have their support stations here. Now is the time to dig deep for that PB or, alternatively, to soak up the atmosphere. Coming up to Big Ben (or as pedants will remind you, the tower of Big Ben since the name refers to the bell itself) you take a sharp right turn up Birdcage Walk to run around St James' Park before passing Buckingham Palace, paying your respects to the Queen, and sprint along The Mall to the finish line.

Spectators should be prepared for crowds, and it's common for tube stations to be temporarily closed so travel is not easy. If you're attempting to spectate with kids in prams, study the tube map in advance to pick the stops suitable for wheelchair access. Avoid lugging pushchairs up crowded steps. The event has an official app to track people but don't be surprised to encounter coverage issues when thousands of people frantically refresh their screens. A relative at home texting updates from the website can be more reliable.

Runners should be aware of how frequently water stations arrive. You do not need to take a drink every time and, if you do, you'll likely die from hyponatremia. Avoid the bottles underfoot as it's not uncommon to fall down after slipping on them.

Pre-race Exhibitions – The First Expo

Expos are either an amazing experience, very much part of the marathon weekend, or a complete waste of time. For the runner, the main goal is to collect a race bib. Most marathons post them, taking advantage of the Royal Mail which has *only* been around since 1516. London Marathon, and some others, don't trust this new-fangled delivery system and prefer that all 40,000 runners trek to the Expo to collect them in person.

Your first Expo will feel like something special. Anyone can run parkrun or pop along to a local race, but only proper runners in proper events get to attend such a massive exhibition just to collect their race number, taking time off work to do so, perhaps requiring special travel arrangements to attend along with seemingly every Lycra-clad person in a 200-mile radius for some quality queue action.

When collecting your number for London, don't forget your VLM registration email, and some ID. VLM allow you to collect someone else's number too, but you will need a copy of their ID, their email from VLM and an authorising letter. Why someone might pass up the opportunity to attend in person may become clear.

Once you have your number you're going to visit every stall since you never know which one might be selling that vitally important performance enhancer that will make all the difference. Eighteen weeks of solid training are as nothing in comparison. A new belt for your gels? An innovative sports supplement endorsed by someone you vaguely know was once good at running and you might have seen on the telly? They're all there, just whip out your credit card.

If you're lucky there will be motivational talks and last-minute advice from running celebrities. There won't be enough seating, so you'll lean nonchalantly against a pillar, listening to advice on pacing and recommendations on what to wear. At some point you'll panic that you don't have a peaked cap. You've never needed one before but the fella on stage said it would be sunny tomorrow and he'd be wearing one. He's a pro so, of course, he's right, and you're an idiot to contemplate running without one. Run to the nearest hat stall and part with some money. Phew, crisis averted!

You pose for selfies with backdrops of landmarks, fill in cards on why you're running, and pin them to a motivation wall. You try on training shoes, all guaranteed to be faster than your current ones. In fact, some of these shoes are so 'unique' you can only purchase them here. As they're not available in shops you'd be mad to miss out.

This carries on for many more hours. The bag of freebies when you registered is now groaning with not-so-free stuff.

After a long day you return to your home, or hotel room, laden with purchases and two new pairs of trainers (you might as well do this properly) and, around this point, realise you haven't eaten anything after that manky hot dog that cost the price of a meal for two. You probably feel a bit dry as well, as you only had two cups of stale coffee and a free taster of rancid smoothie.

Well done, you've successfully spent eight hours

on your feet, barely sat except for the train ride, and finished the day tired, hungry and dehydrated. In addition, you are now contemplating running the most important event of your running career in new gear from new manufacturers. Ideal marathon preparation for tomorrow?

On a more serious note, your first Expo will be great, but you really need to limit the damage. Enjoy it, but don't let it ruin what you've trained for. Your marathon experience is based on miles in the legs and your condition and attitude on race day. No amount of go-faster socks or gels will improve on those.

Pre-race Exhibitions – All others

You will find someone else who is going and ask them to attend a run-down hall in the arse end of town to collect your number. You spend the day at work or home, hydrating and sitting as much as possible, knowing your tried-and-tested race gear is laid out on the spare bed ready to pin your number on. If you must attend you navigate the crowds like a ninja and are out quicker than a cash-strapped investor on *Dragons Den*.

Fund-raising for Charity

Sooner or later you'll end up running for charity, like so many at London. This can be genuine motivation with a charity close to your heart, or simply a means of getting to the holy grail of running places, the London Marathon. Don't take on the charity responsibility lightly. They have to buy their places from the organisers, and must set steep sponsorship targets to make any income.

One issue with raising money by marathon running is how 'easy' some celebrities make it look. The comedian Eddie Izzard ran 27 marathons in 27 days for Sport Relief. He's a slightly tubby middle-aged entertainer. You're a young and lithe athlete in the making, in your head at least, on the cusp of being discovered as the next great running talent for Team GB.

Having accepted a charity spot for London Marathon you face the task of raising £2,000–£3,000. Cue lots of conversations in office:

'Would you sponsor me, please, Phil?'

'Sure, what are you doing?'

'I'm running a marathon!' Cue expectant pause for them to be amazed.

'Oh, cool, I saw that funny bloke off the telly run like 30 or something in a couple of weeks. How many are you running?'

'Just the one.'

'He ran his through South Africa. Temperatures were over 40°C in blazing sun. Are you running somewhere like the desert or maybe a jungle?'

'Not really, no. It'll be nice smooth tarmac in a temperate climate. If you come to watch you might need a light jacket.'

'I expect it's a really challenging course then. Running up a mountain road, self-supported, carrying all your gear on your back?'

'No, it's basically flat. There are aid stations nearly every mile and I'm seldom more than a short walk from a Costa Coffee.'

'I guess it's a small event? Just you and the road, on a spiritual mission to achieve an almost impossible time to complete?'

'Actually, there's close to 40,000 people, the course will be lined with crowds cheering us on, typically three deep, and all cheering my name. It's the closest I'll ever come to being a rock star. The cut-off is so long that I could probably walk it. People carrying kitchen appliances on their backs will finish within time.'

'So why are you making such a big deal—'

'Please just give me some money. Anything? I'm in deep to Mrs Blossoms' Aardvark Sanctuary and they mean business.'

'But you're only running a—'

'THEY KNOW WHERE I LIVE, PHIL! DO YOU WANT THEM TO BREAK MY LEGS? DO YOU? IS IT BECAUSE I WAS SICK IN YOUR WIFE'S HANDBAG AT THE CHRISTMAS PARTY? I HAD A STOMACH ULCER, PHIL. A STOMACH ULCER!'

Given the targets, it's unlikely that you will raise the full amount purely by running the course. Therefore, you'll need to get inventive. The obvious first step is to make the event more arduous with fancy dress. Invite your sponsors to nominate outfits. The more votes the more donations. If you don't trust your friends not to have you running in just a G-string, give them a limited choice, to reduce the chances of your arrest for public indecency.

Other fund-raising options

1. Run more than one. If a marathon is not impressing the people in your life, run two, three or four over the course of the month. For example, a combination of London, Brighton, Manchester, Milton Keynes, Paris can be strung together.

2. Quiz nights. Your friends like drinking and they like showing how clever they are. Find a local pub and charge mates for the privilege of showing how much they excel.

3. Bake sale at work. The highlight of everyone's working day is the dodgy-looking food van that limps into the car park before lunch. Tap into the desperation and sell cakes. Combine with a bake-off competition and let everyone else have the hassle of baking the food while you collect the cash and give the prize for best cake to your mate or that fella in accounts you secretly fancy.

4. Guess the finish time. In the final few weeks scrape the last few quid out of your acquaintances with a sweep-stake on your finish time. Nearest prediction wins 50 per cent of kitty with the rest to the charity. An added bonus is that the shrewder gamblers will start to listen to your fascinating tales of 20 mile training runs in the snow. 'Oh, that sounds a great run, fascinating. How long did that take you? And do you think you'd keep a similar pace for another 6.2 miles or should I adjust my prediction down

a little?'

5. Host an event. Whether a Zumba class, film night or cookery class, if you have a skill or a friend that does, people will part with cash to attend a charity event they wouldn't ordinarily consider. Keep it fun, though. No one expects a Gordon Ramsey rant because their soufflé didn't rise, when they've never managed to make toast without a fire crew in attendance before. If you can cover the cost of a hall or venue you may find an instructor will give their time for free in the hope of attracting regular attendance at their flower arranging/yoga/tantric sex classes.

6. Hold a race. You've probably made a lot of new friends running. Runners like races and some have seemingly unlimited budgets when it comes to race entry costs. Look at what's local and do something different. This could be a traditional 10k race with assistance of your clubmates to marshal, or a hellish event up a muddy hill. Look into insurance and permission from landowners etc. At the other end of spectrum, target the stupid races that no one else puts on. Beer mile (chug a beer, run a quarter mile, repeat four times) or a doughnut race (same principle but with doughnuts). A race will likely take more organisation than other options but could be sufficient to meet your entire target and avoid having to sell your body down at the docks.

London Marathon – 'THE' Marathon and annual rejections

For many, London is THE marathon. Run any other event and it's likely at least one non-runner will ask how long that marathon is, and if it's shorter than London which is THE marathon. It's annoying but, given that the word 'marathon' is these days most often used for endless sessions on Netflix, it's not hugely surprising.

London is so over-subscribed they can't simply open applications to anyone. Their server would fall over as the Glastonbury festival's often does. Instead, Virgin Money London Marathon (VMLM) opens a ballot system for the subsequent year, normally a week after the marathon has been run, and allows interested runners to register. You get the option of paying your entry fee up front and donating it to charity should you miss out, or holding onto your cash and paying if you get lucky. Six months later you find out your result. Why it takes so long is unclear when other events complete the process in weeks.

If you chose not to donate your fee you need to check post box and email as VMLM advise 'A random selection of approximately half of unsuccessful applicants will be sent the Commiserations [loser] magazine and the remainder will be sent an e-zine version. Overseas applicants will be contacted via email'. If you did donate your fee then as a 'Thank You' you'll find the loser magazine is accompanied by a loser top to wear on your training runs so everyone knows you're a loser too and you can share mutual disappointment.

Here's a few stats to ease the pain if you receive a 'Dear John'.

The ballot system up to 2016 closed after 125,000 applications, which meant setting your alarm for an ungodly hour to get up and get in. Assuming you had access to the internet, and were not stuck working nightshift, this was broadly fair as only the keenest got in before the limit was reached. This system was changed and entry is now open for several days. For the 2016 marathon 247,069 applied, for 2017 it was 253,930 and 2018 saw a staggering 386,050 applications.

The organisers are a little vague on how many ballot spots are available but 17,000 is a reasonable estimate and the general consensus among runners. This sounds a lot but equates to only a 5–7 per cent chance under the new system, or 13 per cent under the old.

If you've been unlucky in the London ballot there are other options.

CHARITY PLACES: 15,000 spots are allocated to charities, who are charged as much as £800 for each place. For this reason, they must ensure a return. Runners pledge to raise a minimum sum of money typically £2,000–£3,000 although some can be lower at around £1,000. None of these sums are inconsiderable and, unless you hang out with drunk stockbrokers, unlikely to be raised easily. Months of bake sales, pub quizzes and harassing colleagues may be required, when you'd really rather be training or getting on with life.

CLUB PLACE: VMLM allocate around 1,000 spots to British Athletics affiliated clubs. The number allocated per club depends on the number of registered members (typically at least 50 paid-up members). It's left to the clubs to allocate, and most require you to be a first-claim member (to avoid runners joining multiple clubs) for at least a year, and have already been unsuccessful in the main ballot. Some will take your word, others will want to see evidence, so it's worth keeping your 'loser' email and magazine. The chances in the club ballot can be a lot higher than the main ballot, depending on how many applied and how many got places elsewhere.

GOOD FOR AGE (GFA)/CHAMPIONSHIP: The application process for London confirms the time required to complete a previous marathon (or half marathon in the case of Championship) to qualify for the race, and are split by age and gender, and under regular review. The cut-off for males aged 18–40 was dropped previously from 3h10m to 3h05m and much wailing and whining was heard on the internet forums.

In 2018 the organisers decided to really mix it up. Not only did they drop the male times further and adjusted age brackets to match the other Marathon Majors but also changed the qualification procedure entirely. Previously, anyone under the qualifying time was guaranteed a place. Instead they fixed entries at 3,000 of each gender, filled by fastest runners first in a similar approach to Boston Marathon. This makes for a very competitive field but can mean being a minute or more under your target is still not fast enough to secure a spot.

For London there's also an annual whinge from those males failing to make the GFA limits regarding how 'soft' they consider the female targets. The typical 10 per cent physiological difference between males and females isn't used, and the targets are now closer to 25 per cent slower for women than men and therefore deemed by some as unfair. The argument is irrelevant unless you're considering gender reassignment and, if it encourages more women to take up running, it's only a good thing. Better to live in a world where Paula Radcliffe is a role model than a vacuous TV celeb with an orange face.

If you don't get in for a number of years and don't select to donate the entry fee, then, after six or seven rejections, you might consider 'buying' a spot from a charity with your saved funds and raising money for a cause that means something to you.

6

MILTON KEYNES MARATHON
2012 – NUMBER 3

In the week after London I did a few short runs, turning up at the club wearing my one-size-fits-nobody cotton tee that London gave out. I took it steady, chatting and thanking the coaches for months of putting up with my whingeing and moaning, but it was also a recovery run, something I have come to swear by after marathons.

The morning of the inaugural Milton Keynes Marathon arrived with biblical levels of rain. Milton Keynes is a well-planned town with regard to water courses and drainage, so heavy rain is not normally an issue. Sadly, these torrents were on a different scale and large puddles were everywhere. Huddled in what little shelter the MK Dons football stadium afforded, I shivered with my clubmates, clothed in the latest in wet-weather gear: a MK recycling sack with holes for arms and head. Leaving it as late as possible, we fumbled our way to the very exposed starting area on the road.

At the back of my mind I was considering pace. On a high after London, I believed that 3h54m had been comfortable. Could I go faster? I printed out two pace bands, one for 3h40m and one for 3h45m and, with youthful ambition, set off for the faster one.

The starting claxon sounded and we squelched and squished our soggy way forward. The rain hadn't eased, so I kept the sack on, hoping it would keep me partly dry. The course featured a small section of road before turning off onto the redways, the wide and mostly flat foot and cycle paths that cross the main roads of a town that, one day, must be reclassified a city given its size, using bridges and underpasses. Heavy rain was frequently too much for the drainage system, and runners diverted up banks or attempted Greg Rutherford long jumps to keep their feet dry. Had we known how wet the rest of the course would be I doubt we'd have bothered trying to avoid the inevitable.

Friends and family wishing to support either thought better or retreated to the few unflooded underpasses. This meant there was little noise for most of the course, and only moments of darkened cheering as we passed though.

The rain didn't ease and the organisers diverted one section of the course when it became impassable, adding a few hundred yards. I'm pleased they had the presence of mind to do this, although it brought them criticism, as others would have panicked and cancelled.

As the race wore on my legs tired. Neither the London Marathon nor the drenching helped, but my over-ambitious pace was the main culprit and I began to slow. Even frequent cheering appearances from Cloë and friends (between visits home for clothing changes) were not enough to stop the decline. I was passed by clubmates, and club coaches, and failed to keep up with my boss who was running his first and only marathon. This event proved to be the polar opposite of London: as each mile went by, I fell further behind.

Around 18 miles I accepted I'd missed both my targets and, trying to predict if a time under four hours would be possible, was surprised to find my foolhardy first half had given me enough minutes in the bank to scrape under 3h55m.

The remaining miles were similar to Luton in that I gritted my teeth and did what I could to slow the decline. I was now so wet that I ran the shortest distance possible irrespective of how far up my shins the puddles were. When you're soaked you're soaked, and no further water can be absorbed.

The final stretch runs up what is known as Hospital Hill, normally a gentle slope, but with 20+ miles in your legs and an ocean in each shoe, it's a mountain. I stumbled or hobbled beside the other sodden, broken runners and in the distance, saw the football stadium slowly getting closer. Under the final underpass, which also felt like a climb worthy of safety ropes and crampons, and through the car park, I entered the stadium.

On subsequent events, with good weather, the stadium would hold large crowds cheering on the finishers and is a highlight of the race but, on this, their inaugural event, it was a windswept bleak finish, devoid of all but essential staff and medical crew. I rounded the final corner of the pitch and dragged myself over the line in 3h51m.

I'd endured some horrendous weather and more than a few 'why do I bother' mental patches. What sort of idiot pays money to be cold, wet and tired for four hours, running around the town they live in and could run on a dry day for free? Somehow I'd ignored the voices and had beaten my London time to run an unbelievable second sub four-hour marathon in a week. I could retire victorious.

After a slightly shambolic bag collection, which given the weather and it being a first event can be forgiven, I was whisked home to a warm shower and a massive buffet with friends and family.

Dave, who had unwittingly started all this by asking me to go for a jog over a year previously, was there as well. As the guilty party he was equal parts inspiration to achieve something amazing and the instigator of an entirely pointless way to hurt yourself again and again. We shared beer and some chilli while I recounted the agony and ecstasy (mostly the former) in detail. I like to think he was in awe of my accomplishment, but suspect he mostly hoped I'd go for a shower before my stink rubbed off on him.

Milton Keynes Marathon Course Notes

Course notes for MK are tricky, as every year they make subtly improving tweaks. The first few years included the infamous Hospital Hill towards the end (removed as of 2016).

What really strikes you about MK is that it's put on by running enthusiasts. You come away knowing you have been looked after, and eager to sign up for next year. They do a great job of arranging the volunteers in sections over the route, with a good spread of local running clubs or groups in charge. Everything seems slick, from bibs with your name on and tee shirt size (saves the usual lucky dip of whatever is left, like many events where you either come home with a top suitable for a new-born or to be used as a tent). The stadium is open for the start so there are toilets, and plenty of seating and shelter.

One key attraction of MK is the pacers. Other events have varying calibre of runners. For MK they recruit a Who's Who of the running clubs, most with over 100 marathons to their names.

Half and full start at the same time and follow a common route until mile seven, when the half splits off. The route is well marked with the early sections through the city centre on wide roads. You can cheer on teammates ahead or behind thanks to the out and back sections. Once the runners spread out you switch onto the redways and enjoy a traffic-free and scenic route around MK which, unlike the stereotype image, is mostly green and open. The later sections undulate as they pass under the grid roads and along the parks and hills. This can make maintaining your target pace a little tricky but the pay-off is a traffic-free route.

As with any medium-sized event, if you're at the front or back of the main pack the course can be a little lonely, but this is unavoidable without making it London-sized. Spectators can move about by car, but it is easier to cycle to meet runners at various points.

Aid stations are numerous and have water and Gatorade at most, and gels at intervals.

The last half mile or so, runners get back onto the closed road section to run past the restaurants and on towards the stadium. All downhill, this contributes to a strong finish as you thunder down the tunnel onto the pitch, lapping it before crossing the line and achieving greatness/vomiting furiously. The stadium finish really is amazing and makes the end. You'll then receive your medal and drop bag in record quick time in a large hall.

Although it's not about the bling, the medals are great and different every year. My pet hate is big events that churn out the same tired cheap design. Yes, even London some years. Other nice touches are the Legend club for anyone having completed five of their marathons. You get VIP treatment and a separate changing room, the closest you're likely to get to being an elite runner at a major marathon.

7

AND THEN SOME MORE MARATHONS

New Forest Marathon – Typically British Summer

After a few trail events I fancied trying one in the New Forest. Travelling through the area for work, I'd come to appreciate how pretty (and mostly flat) it was. When I saw a New Forest Marathon for September, I thought it would be an ideal weekend away with the family.

We travelled down early Saturday and went to nearby Paultons Park for the day. The children were of the age where Peppa Pig is pretty much the most important person in their lives, so a day exploring Peppa Pig Land was the high point of their year.

The weather on Saturday was unpredictably warm and by mid-afternoon most of the kids were playing in the splash area to keep cool. With a great weekend in prospect, we headed back to the B&B with two tired but happy children. Marathon running can justify, as well as ruin, weekends. Or so I thought.

On Sunday we awoke to lashing rain. Plans for Cloë to amuse the children in the forest and play areas were written off, and a day of keeping dry and warm, with the least opportunity for tantrums, was her best hope. Any plan I had for a pleasant amble around the marathon course was also gone.

She dropped me at the start and I prepared to warm up in the freezing rain. Looking down while stretching, I noticed I'd failed to put on my trainers and still had my (now very sodden) casual shoes on.

There followed a panicked phone call to my heroine. She was already lost somewhere in a queue of traffic trying to navigate the flooded roads to reach a nearby open farm that promised a 'fun' indoor play area, an essential to keep two kids amused on a day like this.

After much apologising and promises to run somewhere above the water table in future Cloë agreed to return and allow me to swap shoes. I was finally good to go.

I say good. There is not much in running grimmer than sheltering under a tree, huddled with strangers for warmth while sporting a range of bin liners.

The race was started by ex-GB athlete Liz Yelling, who had also started the first Milton Keynes Marathon, which was also largely underwater. I was fast coming to see her as a bad omen.

This was my ninth marathon, so I was feeling a little more seasoned and had a plan to break 3h45m.

As we set off from New Milton town centre, I checked my pace band and rigidly stuck to pace, hurdling puddles as necessary. When the course left town some of the road sections were more like wading across a stream. Logically, the rain had to stop as there simply couldn't be any more moisture left in the clouds. The clouds ignored this logic and kept on raining. Within a few miles I was soaked through and focused on reminding myself that I'd got through the Milton Keynes Marathon in worse conditions.

I'd been expecting a closed course but, sadly, this wasn't the case. We ran on the edge of roads, sometime against the flow of traffic, sometimes with it, and drivers weren't keen to slow and enjoy the view. Around mile ten I started to drift on the pace and had a 'why do I bother' moment. Around the same time, a Volvo underestimated his width and clipped me with his wing mirror as he sped past. Alarmed, I stepped in a huge pothole hidden by the flooding and fell face first, letting loose an inventive stream of swear words.

Lying in the puddle felt oddly calming. I was no wetter than I had been when upright and was getting a pleasant rest. I'd hit the ground hard, breaking my fall on knees and face in a manner that would have made my childhood Judo instructor hang his head in disappointment. The cold water was numbing the pain and by consciously keeping still I avoided having to establish if I'd broken anything. I'd assumed the role of Schrödinger's runner, both fully alive and messed up to hell until I worked up the courage to try to stand.

Shakily I rose. Nothing fell off. I had the same number

of limbs I started with. In terms of volume I was probably up on my pre-Volvo condition as some decorative swelling was already starting. Not ideal.

After a few tentative steps I established that I could run although knees and ankles – unfortunately essential in running – were very sore. My phone was in the drop bag back at the finish line so I couldn't call Cloë to come rescue me a second time.

Faced with the option of waiting for a marshal and a likely slow transfer to the finish, or a painful run I went with the latter. Gradually the pain passed and the incessant rain washed the blood away. It's still the only time I've properly fallen in a race, and I blame all Volvo drivers.

Eventually, just before Noah returned to build another ark, the rain let up and the sun peeped through. Sections of the course began to reveal their beauty and some quieter roads meant we could run away from the potholed edges. There were also sections along dismantled railways and through forest paths (although not as many as you'd expect for a race in the New Forest) which were a respite from tarmac.

The highlight of the race was entering one of the small villages to be greeted by shouts and cheers from spectators who were really going for it and even taking photos. Maybe, I thought, I was running better than expected or maybe they were just amazed anyone had stuck it this far. Sadly, neither was the case and in a cacophony of hooves I was passed on both sides by a large group of wild New Forest horses. They may have been ponies but that close seemed as big as shires. The experience was incredible and startling in equal measure.

Around halfway it was clear that my 3h45m target was not achievable. Sodden, cold, and with legs stiffening, I panted over the finish line in 3h49m, consoling myself with a two-minute PB and my first sub 3h50m.

The finish was in a local school, and use of the changing rooms and showers was a great bonus to cold and tired runners. It was a junior school though, so the shower heads were mounted at around nipple height for an adult and it was amusing watching grown men contort their weary and cramping bodies to get under the water, a cruel and unusual punishment. After hailing a passing wife with two soaked and miserable youngsters we headed home remarking how two days could be such polar opposites.

Phoenix Running – Back to the Future Marathon

Phoenix Running is the brainchild of Rik Vercoe, a legend in the marathon scene, holder of several world records for fancy dress marathons, and completer of 100 consecutive marathons on consecutive days, among others. Most of his events take place around Walton on Thames and nearby. Often, he themes events around the anniversaries of famous films so, when I saw the medal for the *Back To The Future* commemorative race, I signed up. The race was held on 21st October, famously the date on which Marty travelled forward into the future during the original film. No hoverboards allowed.

Due to poor diary planning it arrived as my third

marathon in a series of five in six weeks. I'd assumed this would be hard on the legs but was having a storming few weeks, managing to drop my PB twice in subsequent weekends. Walton on Thames was a flat course so I was hopeful this could continue.

As it turns out, a time travelling DeLorean was what we needed on the day. On one of my early training runs with the club, we had ran past Caldecotte Lake on a snowy Saturday morning as an event, organised by a local running company, Enigma Running, was taking place. Some of our coaches knew the Race Director, David 'Foxy' Bayley, and stopped for a chat. He and I had got to talking and I was due to give him a lift this day. After picking Foxy up, I set off on the short drive from Milton Keynes to the start. Over an hour later, having covered one whole junction of the M1, we got back off the motorway and hammered the back roads. Fortunately, it was a six-hour timed event, which allows as many out and back loops along the Thames as you desire. Foxy and I both wanted a marathon. Arriving over an hour later late was not ideal but hopefully left us time to get the laps in. Another example of me not learning from my own advice and leaving enough time for bad traffic.

I'd missed my customary breakfast. It was now 11.15 and I'd yet to eat, but the upside of being late was that my first few overly fast laps must have seemed unrealistically impressive to runners with miles under their belts already.

The course is along the footpath beside the Thames and is flat the whole way except for a small footbridge.

It's a magic footbridge as it grows with each lap to Everest-like elevations.

Gradually the inevitable happened and I slowed, managing to tick off the marathon in 3h43m, or closer to five hours official time. It was mid-afternoon and, having been fuelled mostly on last night's dinner, I bonked badly.

In the UK, bonk is something grown adults did together in the 1970s and babies followed. In US running parlance it's used to describe the sudden fatigue and loss of energy as glycogen stores are depleted. It's a perfect word as you can almost hear the sound of you crashing down to a stop like a defective tennis ball. We need a British bonk!

After a few minutes of medal admiration my stomach awoke and, fuelled with some Freddo chocolate, I set off to accompany Foxy on his final lap. Unusually for him, he ran worse than me. I figured he needed some company, or a reminder of how much better I was: cruel but having been lapped on every previous encounter it was nice to get one my way.

In another small step towards the long ultras that now lurked at the back of my mind, I decided to make the most of the day and run a bit further on my own. Thirty-one miles would be a new distance record for me and would salvage something from an otherwise disappointing trip. Fuelled by more Freddo bars (how many frog-shaped chocolate bars is too many?) I left Foxy and Rik and kept running.

After seeing the same stretch of tow path all day, I headed off in the other direction needing a couple of miles. Annoyingly, now with Cadbury's finest rushing through my body I felt stronger and keener than I had for most of the actual race. I doubtless confused a few fishermen as they saw a runner pass by in one direction only to return a few minutes later, seemingly in a hurry to get nowhere in particular. Finally getting back as Rik was packing up, I clicked over to 31 miles. It felt significantly further than the marathon but a relief to push the envelope a little.

I collected Foxy, reminded him a couple of times how I was so much faster than him and drove home. On the way I also reminded Foxy I was faster than him. And again when I dropped him off.

The rest of the year went better and, in my remaining three marathons, I dropped my PB twice more, finally breaking 3h25m. Four PBs in three months makes you wonder if more miles is helpful or whether you could be even faster focusing on a single event. More than likely I'd choke on the pressure and fall apart.

Tapering

A taiper is South American herbivorous mammal like a long-nosed pig. It is cute but of no use in the lead-up to a marathon unless you can convince it to run in your place.

A taper is when you dial back on the training in the last few weeks before a big race. It isn't a complete stop, but a dropping down of both distance and intensity to leave you fresh and rested come race day.

The length of taper will depend on your programme

and the race distance. For marathons, it's typically two to three weeks. If you get carried away with the number of races you run, then training, recovery and tapering tend to merge into one unscientific mess of miles.

The principle is to rest your mind and body to allow rebuilding of carbohydrate stores. It sounds delightful after months of training but can often leave you anxious, short-tempered and a pain to live with. You've fought hard against your inner demons to avoid the sofa and lie-ins, and reluctantly your body has obliged. Now, when it's expecting to run around the fields before work, instead it is asked to lie very still in bed. It's worse for spring marathons as you've battled wind, snow and hail to get the miles in during the dark winter but now refusing to go use the daylight and better weather.

Make the most of your additional free time by doing all those things you've neglected. Go to the cinema, put away four months of washing and visit those friends and relatives you've been avoiding as they always remark how 'well' (or 'fat') you're looking. Show them your svelte, lithe, marathon body and they'll tell you your knees will be knackered within years as running is bad for you.

Stick to light duties. The week before your big event is not the ideal time to dig up the patio and lay some decking, as you're asking to drop a slab on your foot.

A study into performance and behaviour of experienced and faster marathoners found that those running the event in under three hours typically tapered for three weeks:

- 4 weeks prior to race: 51 miles (peak week)
- 3 weeks prior: 49 miles (but more than eight runs)
- 2 weeks prior: 36 miles
- Marathon week: 17 miles

Don't focus on the mileage as it will likely make you feel inadequate. Instead focus on the run duration, down to 2/3 mileage, then 1/3 mileage for the final week.

Balancing running with life

I'm often asked about balancing running with the rest of my life, and the short answer is that it's never easy. Once running stops being a chore and you've felt the ephemeral 'runner's high' it's tempting to keep chasing it. The clarity of thought and health improvements afforded by even a short run are positive but the opportunity costs are always there. Every minute spent running is time you could spend with family, friends, or working. As with anything in life there is no simple trick or hack to achieve a happy medium that avoids all negative consequences.

If you were told by a doctor you only had 24 hours to live you wouldn't spend it running. You'd go home to your family, take your kids out of school and spend the time with them. You also wouldn't spend it washing your hair, doing laundry, filing your tax return, going to work or countless other essential chores of life. Against all of these running is a far more enjoyable way of self-improving and has the advantage of being relatively flexible to fit around life compared to tennis court bookings, golf tee times or other more formalised sports.

As the kids have grown and joined new clubs and activities, my running schedule has been adjusted to suit. Billy's football now rules out Saturday runs for much of the year, so long runs have moved to Sunday. Charlotte's Rainbow clubs clashed with Thursday night club runs until she moved to Brownies. Having a formal structure to your running helps with commitment and progress but must be adjusted to cope with life.

When mileage increases during your training the time commitment increases. For a first marathon your husband or wife is likely to be far more agreeable to taking up the slack on a weekend morning in your absence than when you're training for your 59th. Fortunately, I've found other local runners with similar family commitments so we regularly meet on weekends as early as 5 or 6am to get a long run in and get back before the kids wake and breakfast is demanded. Before children it wasn't uncommon to still be up at 5am on a drunken way to bed. Now I'm sneaking out like a ninja trying not to wake them.

Similarly, my main weekly run is now a 5am Wednesday tempo club session where I've made more running friends to help motivate each other to run up a hill in the dark before most of the world is awake. This session is run by a rival club, the Redway Runners so I'm one of the few local runners in both camps, like a dual nationality citizen. For someone that didn't want to join a running club I'm now in two.

If work requires you to travel you can always squeeze

in your trainers and running gear to get some miles in before bed, either in the gym or around the local streets. Hopefully your early morning run before work or during your lunch will clear your head, allow you to focus and be more productive at work. You know your running addiction is progressing to new heights when showers at work are on your wish list for your next job.

Where running is most likely to take a toll is on your relationship with your partner. Running when the kids are asleep will avoid missing out on bedtime stories but eats into the adult-only time together. Getting buy-in from your partner needs to be considered and given priority. I'm far from an expert at this. In the rush to sign up to newly opened races I've neglected to check with Cloë before and found in the case of 'stupid bloody races' and associated credit card fees that forgiveness is certainly not easier to obtain than permission. Sod's Law also states that any ballot race entry or waiting list you put your name down for and neglect to tell your wife as you never expect to get lucky, will almost certainly end in a race spot and an awkward discussion about what plans you have for next weekend.

Cloë has been very tolerant of my weird obsession and even joined the journey. Starting a Couch to 5k course with rival club Redway Runners, she quickly progressed to half marathon with many races in between and until the kids were too big for the running buggy we'd both run the local parkrun. On holiday in Spain we jointly entered an oddly located 10k race around the nearby theme park. I'm not sure either of us fully enjoyed the sweltering course in the Spanish sun around the closed rides and deserted car parks but it was certainly unusual. Her plans to run London Marathon were cruelly dealt a blow by a broken ankle. She worked back to half marathon level again but isn't quite at the same all-consuming passion level I am. She always has been the more sensible of the two of us.

8

MAKING UP THE NUMBERS

Brighton Marathon – Marathon 18

Brighton is popular with many who fail to get into London Marathon. It is typically only a week or two earlier, so it fits in with training plans and they really push it as a 'next best thing'. The one area they beat London on is price: it can be eye-wateringly expensive. Even the early-bird price is more than many events charge for last-minute spots and the late entry fee is nearly double that. For this, you used to receive only a medal and a hideous cotton tee shirt useful for decorating in. More recently they have gone in for technical tops. It's worth doing once, but I wouldn't rush back.

This event was to be my sister's introduction to marathon running. She lived nearby so I took the family and my parents as well for an extended family holiday. The size of the group meant we ended up out of town in a quaint seaside village.

Unfortunately, the marathon organisers insist that you attend an Expo the day before to collect your bib, meaning you have to trek in on the Saturday. This moves further from 'lovely weekend at the seaside with a marathon thrown in' and more towards 'another weekend all about bloody running with scant time left for family'. With luck and a rushed approach, you might only squander a couple of hours in a stale-smelling hall, but it's still a waste of time.

In recent years they've added children's races on the Saturday, and a 10k on the Sunday morning before the marathon, adding to the big weekend feel.

The advantage of Brighton for a spring marathon PB attempt is that early April is cooler and unlikely to get the sudden hot day that often affects London – but more likely to get the worst of the April showers. The year we attended, the weather on the Saturday was awful, and we amused the children in the Sea Life Centre to avoid being washed out to sea. I was hoping Sunday would be better.

The marathon starts in Preston Park to the north of the city. On a good day it's a pleasant green oasis in an otherwise unremarkable area. When I ran it was a wind-swept, sodden marsh with little shelter. I spent the best part of an hour under a tree with carrier bags over my feet to keep my shoes at least moderately dry from the soaking wet grass. Fortunately, it's a look I pull off well.

Preston Park is easy to access from Preston Park station and from Brighton, Hove and London Road station, assuming the train drivers aren't on strike. Even when the service is operating, it's worth checking ahead. I drove up to one station, parked and went to purchase a ticket only to find the platform locked. I then had to drive aimlessly, as close to the route of the rail line as possible until I found a station that was open. With some local knowledge I might have fared better, but my sister had dropped out and I was now running the event on my own.

Being the second biggest marathon in the UK, with around 11,000 runners, you need to get to the start early. The 10k starts at 8.30 and the marathon at 9.15. If you're lucky and get there early enough you may encounter some of the colourful locals on their way home and be offered illicit drugs or a swig of someone's lukewarm beer. I declined.

The start is in pens according to predicted finish times, and you should get into yours early if you're keen on a PB. Typically, I entered towards the back wondering if I had time for one more wee. With a current PB of 3h49m and a lot of decent runs thanks to the recent Quadzilla (four marathons in four days), I was keen not to let a relief stop ruin a PB attempt.

Unless you start from the elite pens, the first section of the route is basically a lap of the park on adjacent roads. The first two are very narrow for the number of runners and uphill – not a great start for anyone after perfect splits. Once the final turn onto London Road is made you pass the first mile marker and onto a straight and wide road towards the seafront. Runners spread here, allowing room for passing.

The next four miles are mostly through the town centre but with a few tight turns as the route snakes

118

back and forth. It is too easy to gain mileage if pushed wide. Taking a left at the seafront it proceeds along the coast road for a long out and back to Ovingdean at mile nine. The route gets very quiet along this section and is exposed to the elements. I'd chosen to wear a vest as the weather was expected to improve, but wished I'd brought an extra layer.

As the course is an out and back you get to see other runners each way and, if you're lucky at mile six and seven, will see the elite runners returning to halfway. If you're already faltering it can be demoralising to watch them glide along while you waddle the other way in a cloud of sweat.

Miles 12 to 14 are some of the best supported as you head back into the thick of the town, passing the pier just before half distance. The crowds are great and you can't help but speed up, aided by the downhill section, and wonder how much you could beat your marathon PB by. I was well on target for a great time and looking forward to crossing the line. Sub 3h40m looked certain, but then comes the first trick Brighton likes to play.

From wall-to-wall noise you are ejected onto a quiet road and, between miles 14 and 18, find yourself running on a nondescript out and back. Enthusiasm can drop and the other runners coming the other way, many of them suffering the mile 18 wall, are a foreboding image of what is ahead for you. My times started to drop. I thought I may have overcooked the start and regretted the speed session through the crowds and past the pier.

Just after the mile 18 marker you're back in the crowds, and they get you moving again. Panic over. That was a poor four miles, but now the crowd lift you. You can enjoy nearly two miles of great support before Brighton plays the final trick.

Have you ever dreamed of running around a bland industrial estate? Have you wondered what a power plant and empty car park look like close-up? If so, you are in for a treat while your legs scream at you to slow. The organisers set up music stations along this section but if it isn't the most boring three miles you've ever run then you must run loops of lighthouses for fun. Even though I'd been warned of this section it was hard to maintain motivation and increasingly difficult to keep a pace. 3h40m began to look doubtful.

As you pass the marker for 23 miles you get back to the crowds. You can't help but be psyched up by the cheering and, with only the length of a parkrun to go, it's time to bin your water bottle, and empty your energy reserves on the final charge home. Coming up the line at 3h43m, I'd missed my optimistic 3h40m but had secured a PB.

I was so focused on the finish line I realised too late that a runner in front was in difficulty and doing a perfect impression of a new-born deer, just metres from the line. His legs just couldn't hold his weight and he slid back down the railings yet again. With the runners coming through thick and fast I couldn't get back to him and wasn't even sure of the legality. If I helped him would he be disqualified? Would I? I vaguely recalled that you're allowed assistance from other runners but no one else. Now I'd crossed the line was I still a runner or become a spectator? If I dragged him across and my help ended with his disqualification and potentially months of wasted training, he was likely to be livid. Fortunately, another runner grabbed him and pulled him to the finish, ending my moral dilemma.

Race motivation

Most runners will struggle with motivation in races at some point. Distance and pace are hard to achieve and, if they aren't, you're not really racing, just enjoying a catered training run with a medal. The little voice telling you to stop, that you banished many months ago, can return to remind you how much easier life would be if you stopped at the pub or coffee shop ahead. Much easier than pushing through the rasping breathing, with chafing clothing, on blistered feet. That cake in the window looks lovely and you've earned it. 'Have a reward!' it will insist.

Tell it to do one.

You've likely put yourself under too much pressure to complete what is essentially an arbitrary distance in an arbitrary time when it is meaningless whether you succeed or not. Promotion at work will not be guaranteed by breaking a time target for 10k. You're running by choice and for fun, remember that and remember that you didn't miss out on Sunday morning lie-ins, bedtime reading with the kids or those work nights out just so you could quit and take an early shower. The training has been done, the race is your just reward and you've earned it. In the words of Muhammad Ali, 'Don't quit. Suffer now and live the rest of your life as a champion.'

If you start to flag in a race there are a myriad of

techniques you can employ. Here are some that seem to work for me over the years.

Take a mental audit of your body condition: Working from bottom to top assess each area. Your feet are sore, but they've been worse. Legs may be heavy but no aches or pains, therefore shoes are cushioning well. Breathing is laboured but it's meant to be. If everything is working, pull up your big boy or big girl pants and get on with it.

Break the race into manageable chunks: Running a long distance at a fast pace is hard. Running one mile at a fast pace is possible so just do that. Then the next one. Then the next. Don't think about which mile you'll finally stop being able to meet your target pace.

Positive versus negative mental ratio: One study showed that for every negative thought you have, two are required to counteract it. Reflect on the good portions of the race, or the training sessions where you beasted up the hills and felt like Rocky at the top of the Philadelphia Museum of Art steps. Play your own mental highlights montage in your head.

Competition: Focus on the runner ahead. You're going to catch them before the halfway point. That's a statement not a question. It's going to happen, so let it. After that it's certain you're going to catch the next before the finish line. Accept that fact and get on with it. If there are runners from a rival club, even better. You will simply beat them across the line or, at the very least, be

122

an annoying shadow on their shoulder that they can't pull away from.

Plan ahead: If there's an aid station coming up and you know what's on offer, look forward to it. That drink and snack are going to taste awesome. The sooner you get there the sooner you can enjoy it, so pick your feet up. Salvation is just ahead and you know with absolute clarity that the boost it will give you is far in excess of Popeye eating his spinach.

Take your mind off it: An 'ever present' runner at the London Marathon who'd run every year since the event started, was asked how he stayed motivated. His technique was to find a lady with a nice bum and follow her. Not the most politically correct answer but if you can find something (or someone) to focus on, it can help.

Make a friend: There are times when you'll spend a fair portion of the race with another runner. Work off each other. You may not be able to hold a conversation but it's likely they're suffering as much as you, and some friendly grunting and rasping words will convey that you should run together and push each other when one starts to flag. On a hilly 10k course I managed a PB when a runner from a rival club and I wordlessly paired off, pushing and pulling each other along for most of the race. Never more than a few feet apart we crossed the line together, having left everything we had on the course. Still unable to speak we shared a sweaty handshake of thanks and limped away.

9

FEELING DIZZY

Enigma Track Marathon – November 2013 – Marathon 30

Many marathons wind through countryside or cities, showing you all the sights. This one takes place on a standard 400-metre running track in Milton Keynes, home of Team GB gold medal long jumper Greg Rutherford. If you seek variety, you will be disappointed: you'll need to run the same track 105 times plus an extra 195 metres to round up.

Track marathons aren't for everyone, but they do have a lot going for them. The course is flat, the surface designed to be optimal for running and you're never more than a few minutes from refreshments or toilets. The traditional manual lap counting used by smaller events would not work on a track, so proper timing mats and chips are used.

Typically, some means to allow faster runners to pass slower runners safely is adopted. In our case all runners were to run on the white line between lane 1 and 2, with faster runners moving left to overtake as required. This works well and there are seldom any issues.

On a cold November morning I turned up with a feeling of bemusement at what I was about to attempt. Having failed several times to break 3h30m I was hoping for better today, when I had perfect conditions on a perfect course. If I couldn't do it now I never could.

The runners lined up along the curved start line just behind the 400m line. Using the full width of the track initially, we raced for the first corner and then tucked in behind each other at the turn, gradually settling into some semblance of order as we circled the track.

With my target time in mind I kept to just under 3h30m pace. It felt easy. No ups, no downs, no tight turns made for a steady pace, as my watch confirmed – an amazing pace. I simply couldn't believe how little effort I was expending to keep so far under my target. Track marathons were a revelation. Who knew lack of incline and a springy surface could make such a difference? I held myself back, fearful of going even faster and blowing up.

As my Garmin beeped for 13 miles I was halfway and on for 3h15m. I had this nailed and kept at it. My pace was constant and I could see nothing to stop me. Counting down the laps based on elapsed distance, I could feel the end of the marathon approaching and I was feeling good. At that point I thought I'd best check the official lap count. I could well be a lap out and would look a fool to finish, arms aloft and grinning like a drunk, only to be sent for another lap. Passing the start, I shouted to the ever-helpful Karen, a mainstay of the Enigma events, for an update. I was expecting three, but could cope with four or five.

She checked and shouted back, 'Twelve laps.'

The grin slipped from my face. That was nearly 5k. I'd been expecting three-quarters of a mile, not over three miles.

After a barely suppressed scream I began swearing at my watch, myself, the track, timing chips and running in general.

Those final 12 laps were miserable as they felt like punishment for being cocky. Had I not trusted the watch and held back so much I might have achieved my target, but I was (literally) miles away. Huffing and passing across the line I managed 3:37m. It was a significant PB but a kick in the teeth all the same.

Later I checked the Garmin trace and, rather than the multiple smooth ovals expected, it showed an almost random spider's web of a route, bouncing from one corner of the track to another, reminiscent of a fly on a window.

If you decide to attempt a track marathon I recommend either manually counting laps or use the 'auto lap' feature on your watch, either of which should be more accurate than wishful thinking.

10

THE GOOD, THE BAD
AND THE UGLY

Organising a race of any scale is no small undertaking, and trying to please everyone from first-timers to hardened PB chasers is a near impossible task. A monotonous-lapped course to one runner would be a simple, race-focused course to another. What really sets events apart, and can make or break them, is the organisation. Often it takes a disaster to appreciate just what can go wrong.

Rutland Water Marathon – The Bad

I entered this race with little thought and include it to illustrate how badly organised some events can be, even when put on by professional companies. My family were in Ireland visiting relatives so I had a free weekend to try to get another race in. Rutland Water was not only the most local but also meant I could return via Birmingham and pick the family up from the airport.

By now fairly comfortable with marathons, I turned up at the reservoir near Leicester to be directed to the large car park. Being an early and wet Sunday in November, the toilets and café weren't open, so I joined a line of runners watering the trees. The organisers had warned it was a lengthy walk to the start line, a mile around a windswept reservoir in the pouring rain. I fell into step with some other participants and braved the weather to the inflatable arch marking the start.

Many races suffer criticism due to insufficient toilets, but this event had decided to avoid that issue by having none at all. The ladies who'd refrained from a call of nature in the car park reasonably had expected a portaloo or facilities here. The complaints raised to the staff seemed to elicit little in assistance other than some vague indication that there might be a pub or hotel 'somewhere over there' that probably had facilities. I can only presume the organisers assumed all participants were demodex mites, the microscopic creatures that do not poop or excrete any waste.

As the start time drew near we huddled together for warmth (a familiar theme) sheltering behind the few trees not being used as toilets, wearing assortments of bin bags and disposable tops. It was bleak and the usual enthusiasm at the start was, for many, displaced by feelings of disbelief that we'd volunteered for this.

The race amounted to one big lap of the reservoir and the small inlet used for water sports. Eventually we started and I'm sure more than a few people gazed longingly at their warm and dry car as they ran past a mile later.

The weather was forecast to improve. It didn't. Foolishly I'd decided that as none of my running tops were fully waterproof, I'd accept the inevitable and run in just a long sleeve top. Soaked within the first few miles I barely generated enough heat to offset the cold. This was not going to be a good race as we trod every sodden, mud-splattered inch of the godforsaken perimeter track and delighted in lifting mud-caked trainers over seemingly endless cattle grids.

I'm sure on a summer's day the course is a delight. In November it was more reminiscent of photos of battlefields, and the number of casualties was similar. As each aid station approached, more and more runners pulled out of the race to sit shivering beside the tables. Air cadets manning the stations panicked around them. Having been tasked with handing out drinks and gels to runners, they weren't expecting medical casualties. The large lake afforded no short cuts for vehicles, so the shuttle bus struggled, and a few foil blankets would have gone a long way to helping the poor runners while they waited.

Around halfway I started to feel the effects of the weather and began to flag from only having water provided. Walking the uphill sections only made me colder. It was only the knowledge that I'd probably be worse off stopping and risking hypothermia that made me carry on. The walking stops got longer, the cold got worse, but I made it to the end in just over four hours. The organisers had decided to add a comedy element to the final section by having us run sideways along a steep grass section. The rain made every step a guess. How far would I slide down the hill? Would I finish under the arch at the top of the slope or in the lake at the bottom? More by luck than skill I skidded across the line, and went to find a rapidly lengthening queue of runners waiting in the rain for the shuttle back to their cars.

One runner was in a particularly bad way, and in unspoken agreement we circled him to give protection from the wind, while his friend hugged him tighter than two friends have ever hugged before. When the bus arrived, he was almost lifted in.

It was a miserable event from start to finish. The reward for completing such an awful event? A poorly printed technical vest and a sodden certificate to fill in your own finishing time and proudly display in the nearest recycling bin. For £35 we were provided with very little: no road closures, no toilets, no medal, no sports drink, nowhere to keep dry. Certainly the weather had not helped but should have been anticipated given the time of year. Neither was the need for runners, or people generally, to have some facilities to empty full bladders unusual.

It's only by running awful events that you realise how much can go wrong and come to appreciate the seamless organisation that goes on behind the scenes on good ones.

After this, Rutland Water Marathon went away for a few years and returned recently, with new organisers and at a more attractive time of year. As for me, if that race didn't put me off marathon running for life, I'm not sure what ever could.

LDWA – Steppingley Step – The Good

If you've never heard of the Long Distance Walkers Association (LDWA) they are worth a look. They organise walking events around the country, often of marathon length, sometimes much longer, and most admit runners.

With winter approaching, a few runners from MK Lakeside decided to have a go at the Steppingley Step, a very scenic route through the countryside around Flitwick, skirting the Woburn Centre Parcs site. On a beautiful winter morning, seven of us turned up at a school hall and paid £7 entry. Yes, it really was just £7 each for a marathon.

LDWA routes are not marked. Instead you have a detailed route description to follow. In many cases, you actually follow a person following a detailed route description and hope they know what they're doing as you have no idea what the sequences of letters mean: 'BR at gate?'. We'd agreed to keep together and take it as a training run so set off a little after the walkers, as instructed by the organisers.

The route took in the best of the local countryside, with short climbs rewarded by sweeping vistas over the farms below as the path meanders around the villages and skirts Ampthill. The steps after which the race was named were considerable but located early on the route where they could be attacked with enthusiasm. Aid stations were inside local village and school halls, with tables groaning under the weight of snacks and food. We ate more than our entry fee and struggled to overcome the temptation to stay for just one more sandwich.

Also struggling was my clubmate Rak who, despite having run a few marathons before, did not have a good day and got progressively slower. His usually cheerful grin slipped into a grimace. Rather than leave him to the wolves we stuck together as a group, sending runners ahead on any tricky navigation sections to make sure we stayed on track, thus saving Rak from covering extra miles.

We finally finished in 5h40m, a slow marathon but having enjoyed it immensely. You don't get a medal at the end of a LDWA event but for the low entry fee you can't complain. For me it was also my third marathon of the week, having run one on Wednesday and another on Saturday, with this as a recovery run on the Sunday. Not a bad week of running.

Reading Half Marathon – The Ugly – When mass participation events go wrong

At the start of 2014 I decided I needed to take training seriously to get my times down and, with other club-mates, booked for the Reading Half in March as part of the schedule. It was billed as a perfect PB course, being very flat. Compared to the undulating local half in MK with a steep hill at mile 12 it seemed ideal. Choking back the tears at the eye-watering cost, I set my sights on a 1h35m target. It even had a stadium finish, so I was hopeful of a memorable race.

On the day, I picked up two clubmates and drove down. We'd booked into one of the park-and-ride car parks (at further expense) and rode the bus to the start. It was manic, as the numbers for this event are huge. After stepping out of the bus you are forced into an awkward penguin shuffle as you work through the bag drop and toilet ritual. They had one massive bag drop for men, and a separate one for women. I've not seen this before or since, and I am not sure what the reasoning is. John and I joined the male queue while Sara dropped her bag off at the female tent. We bid our farewells, wished each other luck and fought through the industrial estate roads to find our pens.

Reading sold itself as a PB course. It promises well-segregated pens and sets runners off in waves with pacers. They do everything they can to help you achieve your target. Or so the adverts claimed.

My pen was so crowded I couldn't find my experienced clubmate, Andy, who I was hoping to follow while aiming for the same time. A minor celebrity (the sound was so distorted it could have been a dalek) counted down to a controlled sequence of staggered starts that didn't actually happen. By poor management or bad communication everyone set off at the same time, straight into the back of the runners in the previous pen. The course was more crowded than London and two miles in I still wasn't close to my intended pace.

Crossing the start just behind the 1h35m pacer I knew that, so as long as I was level or in front of him by the end, I should still make my target. He seemed oddly relaxed about being so slow against target pace already, and I hoped he wasn't going to try and make up for the several minute deficit in a single mile, leaving us struggling in his wake.

The Reading course is far from scenic. The town is not known for its visual splendour (much like Milton Keynes) but the organisers seem to have gone out of their way to include the blandest stretches of dual carriageway possible in the pursuit of a fast course. Industrial estates give way to residential streets and then a brief uphill section through the town.

For a flat course there was a lot of incline. In later years they adjusted the course to make it flatter, an admission they'd failed to provide the fast course they promised despite a hefty entry fee for a 'guaranteed PB' event.

So far, they'd failed on the course description and the staggered starts, but at least I had my pacer. I trusted him to guide us, and slowly saw us pull back some lost time.

At around eight miles I started to notice that 1h35m was looking doubtful. The pacer still seemed relaxed and, despite questioning by other runners, wouldn't speed up. I wondered if he knew the course and would make up time on any downhills (despite it being sold as 'flat'). Eventually I decided to drop him and push on at my intended pace.

The final two miles or so were along a bleak, desolate, windswept dual carriageway. The stadium and its nearby wind turbine didn't get any closer and I started to regret agreeing to come to the event. After snaking around the outside of the stadium we entered the grounds and I crossed the line, exhausted and well outside my target at 1h38m. I'm not sure if I was annoyed or pleased to see the 1h35m pacer looking a lot less smug and a lot more exhausted as he flopped over the timing mat after me, nearer to 1h40m. I appreciate pacing is not easy (I've done it for clubmates) and a volunteer role, but I think we'd all expect to be paced closer to target than that, or at least have an admission that the pacer was struggling with injury or similar and told to push on without him or her.

The race was over. I'd been promised fast and flat with a proper start. Reading had failed on all three counts. The massive medal handed to me went some way to make up for it, and at least nothing else could go wrong.

A few clubmates were waiting in the stadium. I joined them to support the others as they finished, and get a group photo. Leaving the stadium, we bumped into a line of people. Figuring they were queuing for food or toilets John and I cut past and walked towards the baggage tent with our emergency blankets wrapped tight, but it turned out the queue had been for the baggage. In disbelief we joined the back and quickly began to cool. After ten minutes, Sarah joined us having barely waited in the women's baggage tent for her kit. We'd not moved and just as the stadium had never seemed to get closer in the final mile of the race, neither did the baggage tent now. Watching all the females nip into their tent, to return warm and dressed, did little to improve the general mood.

Nearly two hours later we reached the front when I

was quite possibly on the edge of hypothermia. I would have asked for medical help had there not been several thousand others in equally dire straits. I'd already stripped off my wet running top, wrapped the emergency blanket around and pulled the cheap cotton finishers' tee over the top. It's the one time I'd been pleased to receive a heavy tee and not a lightweight technical top, but it couldn't stop the shaking and chattering of my teeth. It got so bad runners cuddled random people in the line for warmth.

I imagine it's becoming clear that if cuddling strangers is your bag then running is your sport. We spent longer waiting for the baggage than most of us took to run the race.

Finally reunited with our bags we dressed, rang loved ones to assure them we weren't dead (although close) despite being out of communication for most of the day, and went to join an impressive queue for the bus to the car park. Pushing and shoving from the sheer number of people, so close to the road and at times on it, was a real concern. I was glad I hadn't brought the family as I genuinely would have feared for their safety, or at least been petrified of losing them in the crush. I'd been to many football matches and concerts that never felt so dangerously over capacity. Once on board the bus we joined another queue, this time of traffic as it inched out of the stadium road.

As a volunteer at races and a run director for junior parkrun, I don't criticise races as a rule. They are typically run by volunteers, often to raise money for charity and have to contend with all the last-minute changes that the British weather and transport systems throw at them. I will make an exception for this event though. Between the issues on the course and the start, they'd failed to hold a fast event. With the issues at the end I believe they also failed in their duty of care to their customers. Despite all this, their social media feed was an unending sea of self-congratulating positive hype.

London Marathon shows how to stage big events FOR runners. This felt like a big event to make money FROM runners. With the boom in running there are probably sufficient punters out there to sell out every year, even if previous competitors would rather eat the entry fee in penny pieces than enter again.

Later that same year, with no specific speed work and on a whim, I entered the Bedford Half, a hilly, scenic route across country lanes. It's organised by Bedford Harriers Athletics Club and is a small event put on for the love of running. I convincingly beat my Reading time despite not actively aiming to. The line for the baggage queue was three people long.

In the spirit of fairness, the editor suggested I contact Reading for some feedback and give them a right to reply on the issues experienced. After explaining my problems and the likely content of the book they decided the best way to demonstrate their improvements was for me to run it again so I was entered for the 2018 event. Sadly it was never to be as the mini Beast-From-The-East storm dumped snow on most of South England and the organisers made the difficult decision to cancel on the morning of the race. This was certainly the right decision from a safety perspective. What was less well received on social media was their decision not to reschedule the race or refund any race fees. To rub salt in the wound they refused to send out medals to anyone that ran the distance at home despite pleas because 'we simply don't have the facilities to post medals to 15k runners'. As a gesture of goodwill they did give a voucher for a sports shop but of a lower value than many had paid for the race entry. The situation did little to improve the reputation of the organisers.

Value for money – race distance & pacing

As you start to progress in your running you'll likely be pushing for improved times. Maybe breaking a certain time or just beating your boss/partner/idiot from the pub over a given distance. Either way, it's important to consider the distance and the line you take. Races tend to fall into one of four categories:

> 1 – MARKED RACING LINE: Only the biggest events such as London Marathon will have the racing line marked on the ground. This is a dotted or dashed line sprayed on the route that marks the shortest possible path around the course and if you manage to follow exactly will give you the marathon distance and no further. The route will also have mile markers and often timing displays, so you don't need your own watch or can make do with just a simple stopwatch. Hopefully you know what your target pace feels like and will hit every mile marker in multiples of that distance. It's easy to calculate

if your pace is 10, 9 or 8minute/miles but there's slightly trickier mental maths involved at 8:37 pace.

2 – MILE MARKERS ONLY: Large city events tend to have every mile marked on course, as accurately as the streets allow. It's up to the runners to look ahead, anticipate the course and try to avoid any extra distance. If using your own watch to track distance it's worth checking at each mile marker as your GPS may over-read. There's no point celebrating finally breaking your target time for a marathon 500 yards before the finish line so pace yourself by the markers. If your watch displays current pace it may mean you need to run slightly faster than your target pace to hit each marker by your expected time; a short 9 minute mile is more like a 9:10minute/mile on the course.

3 – NO MILE MARKERS: Small-scale events typically don't have resources to mark every mile. The route itself will be marked and marshalled and it's up to you to pace for the distance. Smaller events are often cautious in their measuring since they won't have gone to the expense of a full measured certified route so often the route is intentionally over 26.2 miles to ensure it's a valid event. Add some extra distance for weaving and GPS inaccuracy and you're likely to measure closer to 26.5 miles on your run. Don't moan to the Race Director, just be prepared to pace with that distance in mind.

4 – LAPPED COURSES: Needs a little more planning but if the race instructions confirm the lap distance you can calculate time for each lap based on target pace. Then just break the race down into chunks and run them. In a lot of instances there will be a mini lap/extra bit before or after the laps to make it exactly race distance which is a little trickier to factor.

All this can seem exceedingly geeky but run an extra half mile on a marathon (easily done with crowds and a wide course) and that's five minutes extra on a ten-minute pace. If you're busting your arse to break 4h30m you'll have probably blown it simply by wandering on route or relying too much on your own GPS measurements. It's more relevant where there are cut-off times in place. On an early marathon I paced myself by my watch to uncharacteristically near metronomic precision to come in just under the cut-off. It was only with six miles to go I twigged my watch was over-reading and I was nearly half a mile adrift. Gaining that half mile back in the later stages is not something I'd like to do again and was a close-run thing.

Tips from experience

GPS inaccuracies will vary and are adversely affected by very twisting courses, tall buildings and thick tree cover. Underpasses/tunnels will tend to confuse the GPS. Most have an accuracy of 3–15 metres depending on model and, with readings taken every second, it only needs to be out by a marginal amount to cause an issue over the full run. Even as little as a 1 per cent error would add 400 metres to a marathon. It's not unusual to record over 27 miles at London for these reasons.

Assume any city marathon will GPS measure closer to 26.5 miles, and half marathons at 13.3 miles. Pace for those distances.

Assume off-road or trail marathons are closer to 27 miles and half marathon at 13.5 miles on your GPS. Pace for those distances.

The longer the race the greater the extra mileage will be. No one cares if a 100-mile race is 102 miles but they'll kick up a stink if the local 10k is closer to 10.5k.

If time is vital print off a pace band (there's loads on the internet) for the given time, and you'll have a handy check on your wrist of target time for each mile marker.

Watches can die, fall off or otherwise go crazy. Where able, have some backup. Note the time you finally cross the start line at London. If you're aiming for four hours and crossed the start line after ten minutes then you're aiming for 2h10m race time on the halfway gantry as you pass under and 4h10m on the finish gantry. Good luck working out the maths for 22 miles!

If loved ones are waiting for you don't forget to warn them of the likely delay at the start. The bigger events can take as long as 20–30 minutes for every runner to get across the start line. That's more than enough delay for your better half to panic and assume you're in difficulty or been trampled in the herd. Spectating at events is stressful enough without wondering if the life insurance is up to date.

Really big events will often have staggered starts to

avoid congestion, check the race instructions and again warn loved ones or mates of the likely delay. For Paris Marathon Mr or Mrs Speedy setting off with the elites and going sub 3hrs is going to have a long wait for their mate running six hours and setting off half an hour after him. Easily enough time to get the beers in.

11

NEARLY BUT NOT QUITE 3:30

Easter Around the Reservoir – April 2014 – Marathon 37

My goal for spring 2014 was to break 3h30m for the marathon at Milton Keynes. As an incentive I'd sworn off cheese and chocolate since New Year to lose some weight. This ruled out pizza, which for me is practically a food group, so the pressure was on to achieve the target time and start eating again before Pizza Hut went into receivership.

Winter training went well, as did early spring, but my mileage dropped on a holiday to Tenerife just before Easter. There I put in some good hill work and got used to higher temperatures so I wouldn't blow up in the heat of the big day, but most of the runs were short and of a relatively slow pace, so it was all hard to judge.

For my first weekend back I booked into the Easter

Around The Reservoir Marathon in Northampton, consisting of laps around Brackmills Reservoir. My plan was to use it as a training run before London.

The field was relatively small and, as we set off, I was unusually close to the front. Almost immediately we bunched to get through a cattle gate, which is not ideal for anyone going for a PB, but one gate per lap wasn't going to be a huge problem.

Then we hit another gate. And another. By the end of the first lap I had lost count of the gates but it was probably around seven. With five laps left I had another 35 gates to pass. I resolved to just keep at 8minute/miles as long as I could and not worry about the finish time. The aid tables were also typical of small events, 'stop and pick' affairs rather than 'grab a bottle from a long line of volunteers'. It was definitely not a PB course. My Garmin was set to show elapsed time per lap, as finish time didn't matter for this long training run.

When I was a lap in, a couple of runners dropped back. One in front managed to get lost (on lap two!) and we had to encourage him to rejoin us. He was wearing headphones and would have reached Birmingham if he had kept them in.

At one point I was running on the shoulder of the guy in 1st place and felt very unnerved. The pace was easy, I was almost holding back to stay behind him. Could I actually lead a marathon? That was a role reserved for proper runners! I felt like an imposter and almost wanted to apologise to the guy for daring to run with him.

We stayed together, holding gates open for each other

for a few laps until, gradually, I started to slow. The pace was still good, but my mile splits were gradually creeping up. Knowing this was a training race, and being keen not to blow my best performance on a practice, I let it slide a little in favour of even effort.

Gradually he pulled away and a couple of the other competitors also sneaked past. On the final lap one more overtook me and I debated sticking with him, but reason said otherwise, no point busting myself.

As we left the lake for the last time to run the short section to the finish, I was shocked to hear the RD announce my time as 3h31m. I'd finished in 5th place out of 73 runners, a six-minute PB. I genuinely couldn't believe it and felt a mix of excitement that I'd achieved such a time on a slow course with muddy sections and more gates than I ever wished to encounter again, and annoyance that I hadn't bothered to check my overall elapsed time and had let the elusive sub 3h30m slip by.

That morning I learned understanding of the various gates in use by UK farmers and my favourite is now the kissing gate as, with a sideways step, you need barely slow. My least favourite is the latched gate that requires a complete stop and rummaging around to release the latch. I'd also learnt I was a lot faster that I'd given myself credit for, and a 3h30m on a fast and flat course like Milton Keynes, unhindered by ironmongery or rusty hinges, looked certain.

Or so I hoped. In reality, nothing is certain and a disappointing (and slower) MK performance followed, to lead a long string of 'nearly but not quite' 3h30m attempts over the following months. I was starting to despair of ever breaking the barrier and wondered if 3h30 was simply the fastest I'd ever manage.

Competition

The famous and often used phrase in running is that you're only ever competing with yourself. Everyone has different bodies, different aches, pains and life commitments. Unless you're at the front of a race you can only ever race yourself. Throughout my running life though, I've found healthy competition to be powerful motivation.

If you attend a parkrun with any frequency, you'll find yourself running alongside the same people. You won't know if they're taking it easy, when resting before a race or recovering from injury, but you will know whether they crossed the line ahead of you last week and whether it bothered you. If it did you'll push on, hit the hill that bit harder or maybe hold a bit more back for a sprint finish. These are all good tactics and help you improve as a runner. The same group of runners dropping you on a descent every week will show your weakness and where to concentrate to get your elusive PB.

Running with better runners will help you improve. Don't worry about being the back marker as someone has to be, and the faster runners will be glad of the miles on the runbacks. Work at it and narrow the gaps.

12

FINALLY BREAKING 3H30M?

All in for Tallinn? Marathon 45

To celebrate ten years of wedded bliss, Cloë and I decided to arrange something special. Given that most of our friends are equally blessed/cursed with offspring we decided to recreate the stag and hen weekends we'd enjoyed so much, but on alternate weekends. This allowed the mums to drink cocktails in Portugal while the dads taught said offspring to weld/fish/fight bears. The following weekend the positions could be reversed.

This was an ideal opportunity to get a foreign marathon in. I scoured the European list and narrowed it down to Frankfurt, Flanders or Tallinn in Estonia. Having previously popped into Tallinn on a cruise, the boys found the mix of firearms, historic monuments and beer taverns attractive.

To make the most of our time we booked obscenely

early flights out of Stansted on Friday morning, returning last thing on Sunday. One of our party decided the flight was sufficiently early to make sleep unnecessary and spent the evening and all night in a pub instead. There is nothing like arriving at airport security barely coherent and wearing last night's clothes.

With nearly three full days away and a marathon for me on the Sunday morning, it was shaping up to be a memorable weekend. As with many of my previous marathons I hoped for that elusive sub 3h30m but, given my most recent performance, and poor preparation, I didn't entertain much hope.

After touring the town on Friday, we were whisked to dodgier parts for a pre-booked firearms activity. Being ushered into a bunker by two ex-military hard-as-nuts locals, fully tooled up, was reminiscent of the final moments of a spy movie but turned out to be a great experience as we tried pump action shotguns, AK-47s and Desert Eagle handguns.

For anyone wondering, the Desert Eagle is THE handgun used in movies by the biggest, baddest characters as it fires the largest rounds of any handgun. I can confidently confirm they are harmless as the recoil renders them impossible to aim and would be more use to throw at any advancing enemy.

At the end of the session there was a slightly awkward conclusion when we settled the account for the ammo used and the bill was far lower than expected. Possibly something was lost in translation. Should we suggest that they might have undercharged us and offer to pay more, or keep quiet, spend the money on beer and hope we weren't hunted down by trained and heavily armed marksman? The answer was clear.

Later, as we sat drinking the missing funds in a pub it was remarked by Dan how possibly holding back money from trained killers who had collected us from our hotel prior to the event was a short-sighted move. They literally knew where we lived for at least the next two nights. Naturally, we drank some more to dull the concerns.

On Saturday I woke feeling very rough after too much beer and little sleep. If the marathon had been held that day, I doubt I'd have finished, certainly not without decorating significant portions of Tallinn with colourful yawns. After a breakfast and a far-more-interesting-than-it-sounds walking tour of the city, I collected my number from the small Expo held in the town centre and optimistically purchased a 3h30m pace band in the important continental kilometres. We then took in some sights, drank some beers and spent the afternoon drinking cocktails on an outside hotel bar 27 floors up. A strawberry daiquiri huddled under blankets balanced the testosterone-fuelled gun fight from the previous day. After more eating, drinking and climbing countless stairs to admire the view from the church steeple I made my excuses and went back to the hotel extremely well hydrated.

The race set up was expertly organised with efficient bag drops and plenty of toilets. It started and finished in the centre of town with a two-lap route for the full and one lap for the half. Later in the day there were shorter distance races and a Nordic Walk (or 'dicks with sticks' as one of my mates suggested). I'd sneaked out of the hotel early, with only one mate having managed to surface and eat breakfast with me. After chugging down an off-brand Soviet energy drink I moved into the start pen just behind the 3h30m pacer, who was tethered to a huge balloon. My plan was to stick with him and see what happened, but he set off far too quickly for even splits. The sensible approach would be to hold back to 3h30m pace. Instead, I overtook, deciding to remain ahead for the race.

After a few miles I settled to enjoy the town, and found myself chatting to fellow foreign runners, swapping bar recommendations and comparing marathon targets. The pace seemed easy and I kept my Garmin on lap pace and time only, ignoring overall progress and aiming to keep each mile below eight minutes. Drinks were supplied in cups so I opted to slow through each aid station, get as much liquid in me as on me, and pick up the pace to finish the mile on target. Passing our hotel towards the end of lap one, ahead of schedule, I was cheered by Dave 'fancy a jog'. It was countless years since he first started my interest in running. Neither of us would have guessed it would lead to him standing in an ex-Soviet bloc country, hungover on cheap beer, keeping an eye out for short-changed skinheads and cheering me on as I ran a pretty respectably paced marathon. Halfway passed and I concentrated on sub eight pace for as many miles as possible, expecting to fade. Oddly, I didn't. At every major turn I looked back to see the 3h30m balloon bobbing along, not gaining on me.

At 20 miles I began to think that maybe I had this.

Tempted to push on, I remembered how close I'd come at Milton Keynes Marathon and how cramp had killed it, so held back to target. At 23 miles the pace was harder to maintain and I concentrated on running form, reminding myself there was only a parkrun to go. At 24 miles I passed the cheer point at our hotel (now all members had made it out of bed) but could feel my calf muscles starting to object. I couldn't come this close and fail again! But walking tours and steeple climbing are not ideal marathon preparation.

I switched my watch to elapsed time and saw that I had sufficient leeway to slow. Attempting to delay the calf cramps, I consciously dropped to 8:30minute/mile pace. The pain didn't go away but neither did it worsen. I was passed by a few runners I'd previously overtaken, which was disheartening, but I ignored them as much as possible.

Coming out of the park with less than a mile to go I checked my watch and began to accept, with disbelief, that it was finally going to happen! Pushing myself up the final slope to the finish line I jerkily hobbled over in 3h27m.

Maybe mojitos and a skinful of beer is the secret formula for a perfect race after all.

After meeting up with the gang we sampled some more beer and an eye-opening tour of the ex-Soviet-era prison. I'm sure that's how all the elites wind down.

Tallinn was an awesome event and well organised. It's a great place to visit and for a big event was cheap as chips with a decent medal and tech tee. With reasonable flights it's probably a net cost saving over Brighton!

13

RUNNING AWAY (OR ABROAD)

Spanish Half Marathon (Mitja Marato del Carme) – Expected organ harvesting

In 2012 we booked a holiday with the extended family to the Spanish island of Majorca. With running now a key part of my week, I did some online research and stumbled across a local organisation that did running tours of some of the best bits of the island, 'Runny Knows', Polensa. After some correspondence on dates it transpired that a local half marathon would be held in a nearby town of del Carme on the evening of our arrival. Johanna, the expat leader of the company, even offered to give me a lift.

So it transpired that six hours after landing in Majorca I stood outside our hotel awaiting a lift from a complete stranger. More than a few people suggested it was an elaborate organ harvesting ring, separating tourists into active and inactive to assure themselves of the best samples. Fortunately, when the car pulled up, I was greeted by the same Johanna I'd been emailing. She introduced me to the Spanish driver and fellow runner, Miguel, who spoke as much English as I did Spanish so we mostly just nodded and smiled. There were no obvious signs of restraints in the car other than a seatbelt, and no organ removal tools evident, so I got in.

Winding our way along the roads we chatted about running and life in Spain, Johanna interpreting. Although Spain has an active running scene, longer events were less popular so regular trips back to the more Northern European countries were needed to target marathon times. They were both far better runners than I, despite Miguel being on the experienced side of sixty years old. He had the sinewy build of a lifelong athlete, baked hard by the sun. I had the pasty, podgy physique of a Brit who hadn't seen the sun since autumn and had never met a pizza he didn't like.

After abandoning the car on a side street we collected numbers and made our way to the start. Like most runners, I typically train in the evening but it felt a little unsettling to be starting a race at 7pm. In addition, I was sweating in the June heat. My six hours of acclimatisation wasn't sufficient.

Johanna and Miguel hared off and soon lost me. I aimed for a more reasonable pace and to enjoy the scenic route around the harbour, through the town and into the farmlands. We received quite a few odd looks from locals relaxing in the evening after a hard day at work, wondering why these sweaty idiots should be wasting sangria time to get back to where they started.

It was a great run, and really showed the standard of runners on the island and the depth of the faster end as they fought for positions. My time of 1h55m placed me in the bottom of the field but I enjoyed the event. Even at that pace I sweated so much I expected to see a shining trail following me like a snail.

It was approaching dark as I crossed the finish line to be greeted with a big bunch of nothing. This was my first race in Spain and I've since learnt that they don't go in for medals. If there are sufficient sponsors there may be a top or a cap or similar, which are of more use to training and running in Spain than a lump of metal hanging on a ribbon. For a British runner used to medals for anything longer than a parkrun this was quite a shock. After sharing cool beers with Johanna and Miguel, which I'd had to force them to let me pay for after they had already refused petrol money, she climbed the podium to receive her trophy in the women's race.

Johanna and Miguel later dropped me at my hotel, my internal organs intact and complete, and we made plans to meet again later in the holiday. I'd run my first foreign race and loved it.

I've visited Spain and the Canary Islands several times since, and usually manage to find a local race to enter. Often, they're an odd distance, or take in steep climbs and descents for the hell of it. They seem far less hung up on specific distances, but also run far harder. Even the more elderly or experienced runners go out hard and hang on, crossing the line as quivering wrecks. For a laid-back country, they take their races seriously, even when setting just an arbitrary PB.

Vertical Subida del Panadero – Tenerife – August 2015

Typical of many races I've run on holiday in Spain, Vertical Subida del Panadero was cheap but hard to discover. I stumbled across it after an exhaustive trawl through websites, relying heavily on Google Chrome to translate into English. By luck, this race was due to be held only a short drive from our Tenerife hotel in Los Gigantes, and on the second night of the family holiday, before the all-inclusive food piled on any more body weight. We were holidaying with our friends for the very sensible reasons of letting our kids amuse each other so we could concentrate on making the most of the free bar, and to share the burden of making the many frequent trips to the aforementioned free bar.

Signing up was easy, paying was the problem. After some painful emails back and forth with the organisers, it became clear that they were geared towards locals. Payment could be made in cash in the town square or by online transfer to a Spanish bank. This would be ideal for the locals, avoiding excessive booking fees. Unfortunately, it was unlikely I'd arrive in time to pay the cash in person as bookings closed not long after we were due to land. A desperate Facebook plea found a friend with a Spanish account who kindly did the transfer for me, and I got an email to confirm I was set to go – or at least that's what I hoped it said.

The race started at 6pm in the town of Tamaimo, a short but twisting drive into the hills. So while Cloë and the kids joined our friends for dinner I bid farewell and promised to be back in time for the kids' disco and to not die running up and down the mountain. Josh, the concerned son of our friends, was alarmed I'd be missing dinner. I was confident I would more than make up for it over the next two weeks.

As my kids doubtless attacked the tiger shrimps I parked up on a back road of a small town and followed the general procession of runners towards the start in the comparative coolness of the hill. I picked up my bib and race top (all for a bargain ten euros) and tried to limber up along with the others. The Spanish take their warm-ups seriously and I've seen runners do 10–20 minutes of running and strides prior to a short low-key local event. The compere on the PA system picked me out of the crowd for a quick chat as he instantly recognised me as a pasty podgy Brit rather than a tanned slender Spaniard. He was very welcoming and friendly, amazed I'd even heard of the race.

Unsure how to pace myself or where to start in the pen, I squeezed into the rear of the pack. The route was an unusual 5,760 metres, with 2,000ft of elevation gain. That sounded a lot with a cut-off time of 90 minutes for not much longer than a parkrun. The race started on a backstreet before taking a sharp uphill section and vanishing into the distance. I presumed another turn was coming up but no, the lead runners left the road and ascended a barely visible footpath through volcanic hills. The surface was largely loose gravel and broken rock and, with each step, they were forced to dig into the surface for traction, loosening small pebbles and rocks and sending them rolling back towards the runners below. Ascending was a combination of trying not to be killed by falling debris from those ahead, and hoping not to kill someone below. In Britain I'm sure the course would have failed health and safety grounds. The Spanish have a more relaxed approach to athletic fatalities.

Despite my lack of skill on hills I'd started sufficiently far back to be gaining on some locals as I slowly worked my way up the field. Keen not to overexert myself I waited for the path to widen on the flatter sections and was rewarded with a lot of encouragement from the locals in near-flawless English. I responded as best I could in my awful Spanglish and tried not to sour British/Spanish relations.

Entering the first aid station as we skirted the perimeter of El Retamar, I felt good. Sweat ran off me but the evening chill and the elevation gain prevented me becoming too hot. Grabbing two water bottles, one to wear and one to drink, we left the town and followed the road to Las Manchas. Local traffic honked and hooted as they went past, adding to the fun of this great rural route. After Las Manchas we left the road again and took to the goat tracks worn into the side of the steep slopes. The lead runners were well ahead, and we had a great view of them strung along the side of the mountain. Given the narrowness of the path and the large, unprotected drop on one side it was a view worth taking only glimpses of.

Eventually the path widened enough for runners to overtake as we reached the highest point of the race. We'd covered just over two miles and, at some point, passed upwards through the clouds, rendering the coast of Los Gigantes hidden from view.

The next section was downhill, following the twisting footpath as it wound down to the finish. It felt too steep to run but I did my best to perform a controlled descent as quickly as possible. My abysmal granny steps were shown up by the locals who leapt past like mountain goats, seemingly unaware of the laws of physics or gravity. Some appeared to almost ski down the loose gravel at an effortless pace while I did my best not to dive head first into cactus clumps or disappear over the edge of the ravine uttering a string of choice English obscenity.

At last the footpath hit the tarmac road into Arguayo and I made up for my awful descent on the gentle downhill finish. Through my relatively lightweight trainers I could feel the heat of the road, which encouraged runners to keep airborne as much as possible. I crossed the line in a time I'd have been disappointed with for a flat race of twice the distance but having loved every aching, sweaty moment.

After cooling off in a lashed together outdoor shower I helped myself from buckets of iced drinks, pulled my sodden map out of my pocket and began the gentler 5k run back around the mountain to reclaim our hire car and join the family for the children's disco.

Taking Your Trainers For A Holiday

Running abroad is a great way to experience a different locale while getting in some new races. The main things to be aware of are that the traffic is likely to come at you from a different direction (after a hot hilly run you don't want to end up as a hood ornament metres from your hotel), and the temperature and elevation will vary from what you are accustomed to. If running through Spanish hills in August, don't expect to achieve the same pace and overall times as a flat run around your local park in wet Britain. Try to ignore your watch, leave it at home or, if you must log every run (like me), switch to kilometres so the pace is less easy to compare to your usual runs and won't dishearten you.

If you have travel insurance, it's worth checking if it considers running to be an extreme sport, and specifically whether it is excluded from the policy. This is more likely in a timed race where some basic policies prohibit cover. It's not uncommon for competitive marathons to be excluded, but any entered for charity are likely to be accepted. In a curious twist, an amateur embarking on a first marathon, putting previously un-experienced levels of stress and strain on their body, may make a claim simply by having been sponsored, while an experienced marathoner entering for fun isn't covered.

Big events will be easy to locate as they are listed on main websites. Smaller events are less easy to find. It's annoyingly easy to miss a local 10k at home due to minimal advertising and largely word-of-mouth publicity but abroad, with websites not always presenting in English, it's even easier to miss an opportunity. To compound matters, every country uses a different website for their race calendars. After the usual Google search, try Facebook and see if there are any local running clubs you can contact. Typically, people go out of their way to promote their own running scene.

14

BONJOUR PARIS!

I'd wanted to visit Paris for years without ever getting around to it, and the marathon seemed like an ideal excuse to immerse the kids in French culture by spending the weekend in the capital city and doing all the tourist things. In my head they would pick up the language and return to school clad in matching berets and fluent in the local tongue. We also booked a few following days at Disneyland Paris to erase any essence of said culture. Having not managed to get a ballot spot for London 2016, it became THE spring marathon for me.

After some great results in the winter, I decided to target around 50 miles per week, with a goal of 200 miles per month. Keen to get faster I threw away the conventional wisdom of mixing fast- and slow-paced runs. I viewed any run that didn't have me gasping at the end as junk miles and aimed to never run slower than my planned 'fall back' marathon pace of 8minute/miles, except on some long runs. Trained coaches will wince at this approach. It's a recipe for exhaustion and injury but, as is apparent by now, I seldom follow a traditional approach.

The first three months of the year went well: I ran 200 miles each month, easily my highest sustained mileage ever, and without injury! My biggest problem was a cold I couldn't shake. In a bid to get the runs in I began 'cheating' on Lakeside Runners and attended a Wednesday 5am group organised by rival Redway Runners and led by Cloë's colleague Jen. Although apparently harmless Jen is reminiscent of the dodgy kid outside the school gates pushing illicit and increasingly potent drugs and before long has clubmates previously focused on marathons starting to consider ultras and other stupid events as 'all the cool kids are doing it'. It also meant despite initial reticence I was now a member of not one, but two running clubs and had to endure a lot of ribbing for being a turncoat or double agent!

For anyone who has not run in France: they don't use the UK 'promise I won't sue if I die' medical waiver but instead insist on a doctor's note declaring there is 'no known reason' why you can't run. This isn't too arduous if you have regular interaction with your doctor, but the typical 'if it's not fallen off it'll fix itself' runner may not even be registered with a GP. I downloaded the pro-forma example letter from the Paris Marathon website and dropped it off at my local surgery as instructed by the receptionist. Then followed weeks of chasing as I was repeatedly told the form was progressing. Arduously, it moved from 'received', through 'allocated to practice manager' and, finally, the week before we were due to fly out, I was invited in for a check-up.

At the surgery, a bemused doctor asked why he hadn't seen me in seven years as my notes showed no medical history. He accepted this could be because I'd been fit and healthy. After checking how many marathons I'd run (72 by this point), he laughed, said he might as well check my pulse and blood pressure for the look of it and signed off for a £15 fee and the strict requirement that he didn't want to see me again unless I won.

The pressure was on.

Accidental 3h15m – Enigma Week at the Knees – Marathon 71

Sometimes PBs come when least expected. In spring 2016, I was aiming for a great time in the Paris Marathon. Rather than undertake a final 20–22 mile training run I elected to do a practice marathon at an Enigma event 2 weeks prior (since I hate long training runs). My intention was to see how close I could get to a 3h20m, my target for Paris. This would be a four-minute PB but, given how well training had gone, I felt it was possible.

I had my usual pre-race McDonald's breakfast on the start line and set off. The pace was a bit fast for the first few miles and I remained in sight of the race leaders. I felt good though, so went with it. When common sense prevailed, I backed off and settled in with legs feeling fresh. I was going well.

With ten miles to go I realised I just needed to keep sub 8:00minute/miles for a PB of around 3h22m, a healthy PB. Things were looking good.

Checking my watch at regular intervals I noted that my pace was still up. I was waiting for the inevitable fade. It never happened. My watch beeped every half mile to show that I was keeping the pace up. Recalculating frequently, I found that my expected time kept tumbling until it looked like a sub 3h20m could be *on*.

With two miles to go I suffered a slight wobble when a stitch made progress painful. I managed to push through though, and in disbelief crossed the line in 3h15m, a nine-minute PB. If I had been a few years older I'd have been knocking on the door of a Good for Age place for London.

On an excellent day at the lake, I was second as I crossed the line. In all the excitement of the running I'd completely lost track of overall position. It was a massive confidence booster and I felt ready to smash myself at Paris.

Paris Marathon 2016 – Marathon 72

My original intention for Paris was to target a sub 3h20m. Given that I'd managed a 3h15m the previous month I felt the pressure was already off, having beaten my spring target. If it all went wrong I would let the 3h15m pacer go, drop back to a more leisurely 3h30m target and enjoy the event.

We arrived in Paris on the Friday and, after the usual

delays, dropped our luggage at the hotel and went off to explore. Cloë and I had signed up for the 'Breakfast Run' on Saturday morning: a non-timed 5k fun run taking in the sights and ending with coffee and croissants in a local square. Cynically, it's an overpriced parkrun (and the same time as the Paris parkrun only a few miles away) but was a great start to the weekend and more like a running carnival as everyone waves their national flags while winding through the streets.

The downside of the breakfast run was that I had to make it to the Expo before it closed on Friday to get race numbers for both the marathon and the breakfast run. True to form, this was on the outskirts of the city in an uninspiring industrial park inconveniently located for public transport, especially when the metro line decided to break down. Fellow passengers sat on the stationary train, headed to the Expo but aware that time was ticking before it closed. Those only interested in the marathon could return tomorrow and fight the crowds. Those, like me, needing the breakfast run race packs endured a variety of alternative metro routes and a long walk to get there before closing.

Nothing says *Welcome to the City* like spending hours travelling on graffiti-ridden public transport to pick up a small piece of paper before repeating the journey back.

More positively, arriving late meant the crowds had thinned and I rocked up to the first of registration tables. Expecting a deep and thorough checking of my medical note I was disappointed to find my £15 letter receiving little more than a cursory glance before being thrown into a box for filing. I'm sure Mickey Mouse could have signed the letter off.

After grabbing the marathon bib, a rather fetching rucksack for the drop bag and the breakfast numbers, I fled the Expo before I could be talked into wasting euros on stuff I didn't need.

I woke up on race day after a slightly interrupted sleep. Not having drunk enough while sightseeing, I'd overdone the fluids before bed and spent too much of the night weeing. Making the best I could of the hotel's continental breakfast I took the metro to the start, feeling relaxed and ready for the race. This feeling lasted until I walked onto the Champs-Elysées and a seething mass of people all coming the other way. My lack of preparation had seen me arrive at George V station, ideally located for the start pens, but not ideally located for the bag drop in Avenue Foch. I had no idea how far it was, but it was already 8.30 and my pen was due to close at 8.40.

Deciding not to dump my bag by the side of the road I realised I'd just have to run for it, pushing my way through the oncoming hordes as politely as possible and hurdling strolling Parisians and their dogs. While in the queue to drop my bag, large display screens showed the elite start going off at 8.45. The cheers as one plucky club runner briefly took the lead lifted my spirits and took the edge off what a total mess I was making of my spring marathon.

The day was shaping to be one of the hottest of the year, which didn't help my panicked and sweaty demeanour. After another warm-up sprint (this time going with the flow) I made it to my pen in time to see the back of the final runner setting off. The next pen was about to be released but, fortunately, a marshal took pity on me, squeezed me through the barrier and I chased them down the iconic street. After nearly ten metres of the Paris Marathon I was already a sweaty tired mess. A casual observer would struggle to believe this was my 73rd attempt.

I held the pace back with a halfway goal of 1h37m, a time I'd achieved several times over the past dozen or so races. The 3h15m pacer was now just ahead and I tried to force all doubts from my mind and the sweat from my eyes, and settle in.

At around five miles the course breaks out of the picturesque streets and enters the Bois de Vincennes park. It's beautiful and largely flat, but I started to feel the inclines. A doubting voice in my head reminded me that I'd probably covered a decent-paced parkrun in the process of getting to the start pen, and kept reminding me how tired my legs were. It also noted how bright the sun was and inquired if I could feel it beating down. Yes, I could.

Each water stop I grabbed one bottle to drink and another for my head. Until the later stages only water was provided, so I had some sports tablets ready to drop in. As the race progressed, my bottle turned all the colours of the rainbow.

Halfway arrived after re-entering the city. I'd kept sight of the 3h15m pacer and my splits were on target, although I was comfortable. All I had to do was maintain the pace, but when the 25k marker arrived I'd dropped off a little.

By then I could have murdered someone for a Red Bull or a Coke. In desperation I tried one of the weird French energy tubes from the aid stations. They looked like travel-sized toothpaste and tasted like the bizarre offspring of cake icing and Haribo. The locals seemed to like them, but they didn't sit well with me and I started to slow. I lost the pacer and had a 'why do I bother' spell. Through one of the underpasses, away from the crowds and spectators, I slowed to a walk.

I wasn't the only one struggling though, and was still passing people despite my massive drop in pace. I felt awful, but not as bad as they looked. Taking comfort from their misery, I resolved to salvage what I could. Some rough sums told me I was still broadly on pace for just over 3h30. Every mile I could press on would pull my time back.

My efforts to progress were hampered at every aid station by someone stopping dead in front of me to peruse the selection as in his local *supermarché*. My French isn't good enough to convey my thoughts ('It's the same bloody stuff as the last ten stations!') so I adopted the British approach of tutting loudly.

Checking my watch at every distance marker I saw that I was just about holding it together. The shortest route on the course was marked with a green line and I doggedly stuck to it, bearing down on the runners in front and intimidating them to one side. For the final five or so miles, the course again left the bustling Paris streets and wound through Bois de Boulogne, home of the Paris parkrun. It is a beautiful area but was sadly devoid of supporters. The few people we passed were out for a leisurely Sunday run in the dappled shade of the trees.

Normally when I'm on a training run and happen upon runners in a race I suffer terrible envy, but right then I would happily have swapped my lot for a relaxed social run along the shaded soft trails.

Wailing sirens brought me back from my daydream. Subconsciously, I had probably registered a lot of ambulances and rapid-response bikes on the course but this was the first time I noticed how many were being tended to at the side of the road. One runner who succumbed was caught by passing runners as he fell, and gently laid down on the road. He clearly was in no fit state to look after himself.

It was heart-warming to see runners jeopardise their race to help but also hilarious to watch the fallen runner slowly raise his arms over his chest and bring them together as if to pray for recovery – when what he actually did was pause his Garmin. You can imagine his tale to his mates: 'Look at my awesome splits for 22 miles, I was on my way to a massive PB until I woke up in the first aid tent.'

While doing my best not to join the stricken runners, I continued dumping water on my head while focusing on the green line. If I could avoid any further slowing I might sneak a time under 3h30.

As the crowds started to build again in the final miles I felt I could relax and enjoy the atmosphere. The spectators were chanting '*Allé, allé!*' for us to go, go. In that curious mental fog you get at the end of the race I wondered who this runner called Ali was and whether it was an Alison or an Alistair, hoping that I'd manage to keep ahead.

Exiting the park, the finish line came in sight, and I crossed in 3h27m. The final stages had been a painful grind but had got me under the 3h30m.

I couldn't help but see the parallels with my mission to set a PB at Milton Keynes two years previously, setting my fast time in a practice marathon the month before. For Paris I'd done exactly the same and peaked too soon, setting a 3h15m PB I might never match at a small-scale event.

After collecting my medal, I did a quick change in the portaloo, consumed my body weight in orange segments and made my way via the metro to the hotel to meet up with my family for our transfer to Disneyland. There is no better marathon recovery than meeting Mickey and his mates!

In total I covered 37 miles that day including the afternoon at the theme park. No wonder my legs were complaining as I squeezed into bed, but I felt that I'd 'done' Paris and wouldn't need to return.

Paris Marathon Course Notes

It's a big city event so allow a lot of time. Number collection is from the Expo on the outskirts of Paris, open Wednesday to Saturday. Collect as early as possible or risk wasting time. If doing the breakfast run (5k fun run) on Saturday morning, go on Friday to collect entry for that as well.

The main items to remember at registration are your ID (passport) and your medical note from the doctor. There is no leeway over this. No medical note, no number, no race, and no amount of tears, tantrums or begging will get them to waive this.

The start of the race is on Champs-Elysées and the street, although closed to traffic, is open in all other respects, which means that you'll be jostling with locals out for breakfast or doing some shopping. The bag drop is on an adjacent street, Avenue Foch, so make sure you arrive at that street first. The going between the two is slow with Christmas-sale levels of crowds.

The organisers use a staggered start to avoid over-crowding. Check which wave you're in. Start times range from 8.45 to 10.05, with pens closing 10–15 minutes before the start.

Most of the route takes in the sights. Mile 6–11 is in the Bois de Vincennes park before doubling back along the Seine. Mile 21–25 are around the Bois de Boulogne park. Crowds tend to thin out here, where you possibly need them most. The Finish is on Avenue Foch, heading towards the Arc de Triomphe. The course is largely flat with gentle inclines.

Don't expect the millions of spectators you see at London, five deep and shouting your name. Parisians are too sophisticated for that, and more likely to nod support while smoking tiny Gauloises cigarettes. They also won't adhere to the route crossings, so be prepared to navigate around a local walking his poodle across your path without a care.

Gels on course are unusual tubes of thick sludge. If

you require the usual liquid gels, take your own.

As you're likely to be using the metro to get around it's worth carrying a spare single use token in case of mishaps.

In common with many other city events the medals are as awful as the plastic medals handed to kids for sports day races. When they're five.

Finally, other running mates have been charged as much as £50 for the doctor's letter, worth bearing in mind if funds are tight.

15

MILTON KEYNES 2016
– BECOMING A LEGEND

One of my favourites on the race calendar, this was my fifth time running the MK Marathon and, for the first time, a two-day event was to be held. On the first day, Cloë and I took part in the 'Rocket 5k', a mostly downhill race from the city centre to just outside the stadium. I failed to take it steady and pushed myself to my first sub-20 minute 5k. Whether this was an ideal taper activity the day before a race is open to dispute.

The organisers had set up a loyalty club known as 'The Legends' to reward runners who have finished five Milton Keynes Marathons. The main incentive was an extra 'Legend' medal, and a VIP changing /refreshment area overlooking the finish line. I won't ever get in a VIP area at a race based on finish time or fame, but I can seemingly do it on sheer persistence. There was a great laid-back atmosphere in the room, with 30 or so runners drinking coffee and chatting. Most were very experienced, so there was little of that nervous energy and doubt often found at the start line. It was more akin to a lazy Sunday morning spent at a coffee house, but with more Deep Heat.

Being a mix of local runners and 100 Marathon Club members, almost everyone knew at least a few of the others so it became a friendly staging area hosted by Kas, the original Event Director and founder of the MK Junior parkrun.

A special guest in the room was Ben Smith from the 401 Challenge, undertaking a World Record attempt to run 401 marathons in 401 consecutive days to raise awareness and funds for charities tackling bullying. He was running his 245th marathon and it was great to meet such a running legend.

With 30 minutes to go before the start, we were taken into the bustle and excitement of the masses and the starting pens. Standing between the 3h00m and 3h15m pacer I found myself in a quandary of what pace to run at. My 3h15m in March had seemed effortless, the 3h27m in Paris had been hellish. I'd suffered the previous night with the start of a cold or flu and even had an afternoon nap. Sensibly, I should run with the 3h30m pacer (the legendary Steve Edwards, runner of over 800 marathons under 3h30m) and push at the end.

I took the less sensible approach of running out hard to get miles banked before the temperature crept up. It worked well, and I banked a HM PB, trying my best to ignore the rising temps and the soreness in my heel that felt like a blister coming. I was wearing my favourite pair of lightweight Adidas shoes which lacked grip in wet weather so had been consigned to the cupboard all winter. This beautiful spring day was their first outing of the year and they'd rewarded me with a burning sensation on my right foot.

On the early out and back sections I saw the lead runners for both the half and full marathon running the other way, and it was great to witness GB runner Steve Way gently amble past to nearly break the half course record. It was a training run for his planned ultra the following week.

A few of my clubmates had volunteered as lead bikers so I received support and abuse in equal measure as they passed.

Nearing halfway I started to struggle. The crowd and volunteers were mostly from Redway Runners and I could hear them chanting and cheering for Jen from their club who slowly reeled me in. I had brief hopes of staying with her but, despite claims to be suffering, she effortlessly cruised by and left me for dust, a feeling I've become very used to. Frequent visits to the course by my long-suffering family extended from a brief wave as I sailed past in the early stages to gentle walks, until in Willen I stopped dead while chugging down an energy drink and they filled my bottle with sports drink.

The rest of the race was much like a re-run of Paris. I'd faded horribly and was looking on course for 3h35m. Having failed to get under 3h30m on my last two attempts at MK I decided I must do better, so slogged it out. My mood was lifted slightly by the number of people I was passing, even at this atrocious pace.

At 22 miles I passed those clubmates who had finished

their lead biking and were soaking up the sun. They admonished me for awful running form. I have since seen the photos: my head droops forward so much I look like I'm trying to read my own vest.

With a final push along the grid road towards the stadium I passed a few more runners and tried my best to regain some semblance of form for the amazing stadium finish. With a bleeding nipple and a fiery heel blister I crossed the mat in 3h26m. It was my 7th fastest marathon at the time, and my 10th time under the magic 3h30m. It had not been pretty or much fun for the second half, but I was seemingly able to achieve on 'off' days what I struggled to achieve on my best only a year previously.

Later, after chatting to some of the others, I collected my amazing cow medal for having run both the 5k event the previous day and the marathon, and went off to find the legend room where I could claim my '5x Legend' medal. Four medals from two days is a pretty impressive haul.

Chafing and Running

This is one of the less fun aspects of running. No matter your shape, size or fitness, at some point or another the simple act of running will hurt more than just your muscles. Chafing can happen anywhere your clothing touches you. Over the course of a run, a minor rough hem or seams on a top can rub and cause irritation. The best way to combat this is to test clothing on shorter runs first, and apply lubricant to any potential rub areas.

For some others it's skin on skin that can cause issues. Thighs rubbing together, or armpits are glamorous areas to rub raw and impede your normal life for a few days. There's a lot of differing options out there, from normal Vaseline to purpose-designed running lubricant such as Bodyglide. The wetter you get, the more likely you are to wash off the protection and suffer. For this reason it's often better to wet your neck, wrists and legs on hot events rather than dump an entire bottle over your head, soak yourself through and make the chafing worse. More than a few events I've seen tight-fitting shorts, often on ladies, rub clean through the skin on front of quads and leave lovely trails of blood behind.

If you're a bloke, then your smug satisfaction at not having to squeeze 'the girls' into a sports bra will be offset by your running top rubbing your nipples raw. More of an issue on wet races or when sweating heavily, nothing ruins a race photo as much as two bloody bullet wounds on your chest. They also put the dampener on post-race showers when you step under the jet and collapse in pain as the water pounds the raw nips.

You will have new-found sympathy for any woman that breastfeeds though. If you've got the body of a god with a perfect six-pack you could run without a top, but for the rest of us it's a case of trial and error – or maybe just join the ladies and try a bra for some solidarity with your sisters.

Some runners swear by nipple guards, some use plasters or surgical tape, while lubricant can be enough for others. I've resorted to duct tape before in a desperate attempt to avoid passing out from booby-related blood loss. Experiment and check, and avoid white running tops. Or yellow. Or blue. You know what? Only wear red.

16

SING WHEN YOU'RE WINNING

If you're very lucky or very good, as most of us are not, then persistence will eventually deliver you a race after which you can stop boring your work colleagues with a finish time and instead bore them with a finish position.

Enigma World Cup 50th Anniversary – Marathon 77 (and a turn up for the books)

This was a unique event organised by Enigma Running to celebrate the 50th anniversary of England winning the World Cup. Starting at 3pm to match the kick-off was a nice touch and meant a decent lie-in. However, it messed up my pre-race routine and I had to substitute a late brunch breakfast in Debenhams café and a shopping trip with the family to loosen the legs off.

As it was a themed event most runners were sporting England outfits and I was resplendent in my £4 England tee from Primark. Being a pro, I knew a cotton tee would not be ideal for a marathon, so I packed a spare club vest to change into on one of the laps. Being an idiot, I packed it with a leaking drinks bottle so it was sodden in sports drink before I started, leaving me a choice of friction-inducing cotton or wasp-attracting technical fabric.

The starting temperature was higher than I prefer but better than a July afternoon could have been. Unusually, I'd had a short taper into the race as I was ahead on monthly mileage. The marathon would tick me over the 200-mile target. I felt fresh and, coupled with a new pair of On Cloud lightweight shoes, confident of holding it together for a sub 3h30m.

Looking around at the other runners, and encouraged by Foxy, the Race Director, I began to think I might achieve a podium finish if I could keep to a 7:45minute/mile average pace. This went out the window as we set off and I ran the first few miles nearer 6:40 with a fellow runner on my shoulder throughout. After four miles we settled to a slightly less suicidal 7:00 pace, and on the second of the seven laps he slipped past and I ran on his tail.

We both admitted we'd gone off too fast but, with the third runner only a few hundred yards behind, neither of us wanted to risk slowing further. Still together on the third lap, he joked we were expending a lot of effort for a potential win that earnt the same medal as everyone else. We weren't likely to get a last-minute call up to the Rio Olympics as a result!

Running for pointless and worthless pride was the only reason we kept pounding around the lake, dodging dog walkers and countless Pokémon Go players, eyes glued to their screens looking for hidden characters.

At the end of the third lap I grabbed a flat Coke to augment the Lucozade I'd started on, and dumped a bottle of water over my head. At nearly halfway I was feeling the heat, wondering how long I could keep at the pace and whether 1st place was slipping away. It was interesting, following alongside or close behind another runner, to see the different lines and approaches taken to the same course. I'd pull ahead on the uphill slopes and lose ground on the flat, regaining it on the downhill slopes. With reminders from a recent coaching session in my head I concentrated on fighting the slump I'm prone to and did my best to visualise a helium balloon tied to my head pulling me up straight. It seemed to work, and I kept with him.

Somewhere on lap four our tandem running ended and we parted company. I started to pull ahead and, heading through halfway in a PB of 1h34m, realised how much I'd overcooked the start. This was either going to be an amazing race for me or one that ended walking or vomiting into bushes.

This train of thought was soon broken by another runner creeping up behind. He'd been safely third from the beginning, paced himself well, and was gaining. He'd already passed my running buddy from the first three laps. It was inevitable that he'd pass me as well, as my pace fell and I wondered if I'd blown my chance of a win by setting off too quickly. When would I ever learn to have confidence in a steady consistent pace?

This guy obviously knew his pacing and seemed relaxed as he pulled away from lap five. The early pace took its toll and I dropped the occasional mile slower than 8:00 pace while he retained a metronomic stride. Resolving to stick with him I kept pushing, fighting the heat and the increasing weight in my legs. Near the end of the lap I caught him when he seemed to have a brief muscle issue and pulled to one side. Back in 1st place with only seven miles left I thought, hey, maybe I hadn't blown it!

The final two laps were spent sweating in the cotton tee and looking over my shoulder. Around one of the looping sections of the lake I noticed my tail was only a few hundred yards behind, which was not much of a margin with five miles left. I kept pushing. Passing the lap point and hearing the bell I was still in front with just 3.5 miles to go, but was fading further and my splits were dire. My potential 3h20m finish now looked closer to 3h30m.

Pulling out my iPod to select some motivational music, I set off again to battle Pokémon collectors, the heat, dog walkers, recalcitrant geese and the looming spectre of the advancing pack behind.

With a mile to go I started to believe I'd finally done it. My 77-marathon plan to keep plodding on had paid off. I could hear the pub calling and almost taste the first pint. My efforts were not in vain and I staggered over the line in 3h27m. Contradicting my earlier thoughts, my rival and I had unknowingly been battling for more than glory and I was presented with a 1st place trophy.

Sure, it was only a plastic replica of the Jules Rimet World Cup, but as the only running trophy I've ever won it was destined for a permanent spot on our bookcase.

17

ABINGDON MARATHON – THIRD TIME LUCKY? – MARATHON 80

Long regarded as the flattest UK marathon before Manchester made the same claim, Abingdon is a popular autumn event for achieving PBs. For anyone who missed the London Marathon ballot it's a chance to secure a Good for Age (GFA), and qualify instead.

A relatively small event with around 1,000 runners, it has a definite focus towards the sharper end of the field. Cut-off is five hours, compared to six or more for most events. Even within the five hours there is a definite leaning towards the faster finish times. A 3h45m run would typically see you finish in the top 20 per cent of finishers in most races. Here, it's more likely you'd be in the bottom half or lower. It also strictly enforces the UK Athletics ruling on headphones, and if a marshal spots you using headphones you will be disqualified and listed as such in the results. There is no sense in running a world record pace only to have it voided.

The event is held in October, with registration opening in February and typically filling by April, so it's worth keeping an eye on their website. It starts and finishes at Tilsley Athletics Stadium. The event has a great 'small but organised' feel, and benefits from a fair amount of indoor area to keep warm before you start, and showers with changing facilities afterwards. The downside is that parking is located a fair walk away. This is not a huge issue unless you're running late, in which case the ten-minute walk will turn into a run.

After the first five miles through the town, you begin the first of two eight-mile loops, after which the course follows a three-mile route back. Given how scenic the surrounding countryside is, you could be forgiven for expecting some spectacular sections. Sadly, in the interests of keeping the elevation down and providing a flat course, it is by and large dull, taking in business parks and residential streets. The few sections along the River Thames help, and the tour past the Tudor buildings provide relief from what is an unremarkable course, but most people are there to run a good time, not have a good time.

I first ran the course in 2013, on the hunt for a PB. Following a 3h43m at Brighton in the spring I'd had some disappointing results over the summer and intended to make up for it. True to form I'd been swept along by unbelievably quick runners, posting a brilliant time for the first half before falling apart. Climbing up the underpass in the last few miles I realised I'd missed it. I pushed on for the finish through cramping legs, swearing at the seemingly pointless loop of the park before hitting the athletics track and pushing for home, managing a 3h45m. It was my second quickest but felt a long way behind the Brighton time. Consolation of a sort came with the realisation that in only two years I'd gone from barely finishing my first marathon to mixing it with the proper runners – albeit at the back of the race.

Come 2014, I returned to do justice to the course. I'd spent a year training hard, narrowly missing a sub 3h30m and gaining a 3h31m PB on a course with gates and cattle grids, having gone sub 3h35m a few times in the previous few months. This course would be quicker, and I felt certain of a sub 3h30m. The main difference on my second visit was the number of other runners I recognised from previous events. We were like a Marathon Addicts Anonymous. Lining up on the track again I planned to run conservatively, saving something for the second half but, when we started, I once again got swept along, and had to check my watch to consciously slow the pace. It didn't help and 3h45m later I was back on the track, crossing the line 1 second slower than 12 months previously, a monumental disappointment for a year of training.

I didn't bother running in 2015 and instead took a year away, ready to return in 2016 and finally get that PB. Having secured a 3h15m earlier in the year and a 3h24m only a few days after another marathon I was feeling pretty good. Only a grumbling ache in a calf gave any concerns, so I started wearing calf guards (the funky compression wear for your legs you hope will magically fix them).

Abingdon maintains an old-school feel by serving water in cups, with two stops serving sports drinks in bottles as a concession to the modern desire for sugary go-go juice. For this reason, I ran with a soft bottle of sports drink in my shorts to help me through. The first half went well as I kept pace with clubmate Dionne, who was worried her back injury would return and force her to quit. She maintained pace and went on for a 3h15m finish. Jealous, *moi*?

I started to fade. My grumbling calf caused me to run a little off and my ankle was whining. I hadn't remembered, but the course has countless cuts on and off pavements and along crumbling footpaths which break your stride, reminding you of all those aches or pains that had been temporarily forgotten.

With about eight miles to go I was doing my usual mental arithmetic. How slow could I go to salvage a sub 3h30m? I'd also been reminded how uninteresting the course was. With my 100th planned for 11 months hence, if I could keep it under 3h30m I'd consider the event 'done' and never need to return. That was a massive incentive.

As much as I was trying to run a tight line the course was coming up as a little long, around 0.2mile extra, but that was manageable. Then I hit the 21 mile marker and was suddenly half a mile out, according to Garmin? How had I gained so much in a single mile? How badly had I been weaving?

If the marker was right I'd be finishing at 26.7 miles. That extra half mile was costing me the 3h30m.

I nearly threw the toys out the pram and walked but, just in time, saw the 22 mile marker and the error drop back to 0.2 miles. I hadn't managed to misplace myself, it was the marker that was misplaced, so I could concentrate on pushing along.

Coming up the slope to the Tilsley stadium entrance it was still too close to call. If I had to make the heartbreaking lap of the adjacent playing fields I would be outside my target time but, luckily, the route was slightly revised and we ran straight into the stadium for a lap of the athletics track. My right leg was grumpy at this point so no sprint finish was in the offing, and I jerkily hobbled in at 3h28m.

Abingdon was 'done' and I wouldn't need to return, especially after being presented with a thoroughly dodgy green technical top that makes the wearer resemble a scout leader, or worse, someone pretending to be a scout leader.

18

COMPLACENCY – BOURNEMOUTH MARATHON FESTIVAL 2016 – MARATHON 81

Bournemouth started its running festival in 2012 and has been a slick operation ever since. At the start of October, it seems to hit the final few days of summer and makes a great weekend away. Races range from 1.5k for six-year-olds to marathon distance, so it's a very inclusive weekend, great for running clubs with different level and distance targets.

Aside from the children's races they have a 10k on the Saturday afternoon, followed by a 5k in the evening, scheduled to be run mostly in the dark with entrants encouraged to wear lights and fancy dress. Both start and finish by the main pier so are great for supporters to cheer on their friends. It also means it's a very relaxed 'Please hold my hoodie and valuables dear wife/

189

husband/honest-looking stranger, I'm just off for a race and will be back shortly to amaze you with my medal' affair. The running is more a fun part of the weekend than an all-consuming nuisance.

The Sunday has a half marathon starting at 8am, and a full marathon at 10am. Both start at the nearby Kings Park (also the site of Bournemouth parkrun if you fancy a Saturday warm-up). What a few people have realised is that the programme allows a keen/foolish runner to enter all four main distances.

In Year 1, I ran just the marathon, while supporting clubmates in the other distances. I was passed by far more of them than I anticipated, due to dodgy pacing.

In Year 2, I again ran just the marathon but suffered terrible envy watching the other participants running the Saturday events in the late summer sun.

In Year 3 I awoke on Friday at home, unable to ground my right foot as a niggling calf issue had turned into a solid lump of uncooperative gristle overnight. I hobbled from the car to the sports shop for a leg roller and did what I could to coax some life back into it, resolving afterwards to head down for the weekend anyway. The rest of the family were keen for a weekend on the coast, so I'd see how the leg stood up before committing to the marathon. On Saturday morning it felt stiff but better. When I tried a tentative trot at the parkrun it seemed to be operational.

In the afternoon a space in the 10k event became available. I decided to use it as a final check on the leg, and had one of my most enjoyable races ever. The course was amazing and the crowd support awesome, especially as

I was bedecked in a Superman top and cape. Running well within yourself and enjoying the experience cannot be recommended enough. Not every race has to be a flat-out effort.

Spurred by the success of the 10k I went on to run the full marathon the next morning, after my usual cooked breakfast. Given it was a third marathon in five weeks I was only aiming for an acceptable time, but I benefited from a second wind on the final seven miles or so, picked up the pace and managed a surprise PB. This got me into the mindset that a warm-up event on the Saturday was a good idea. Emphasis should have been on 'a' warm-up event rather than 'several'.

For 2016 the Redway Runners returned en masse to Bournemouth. It would be my fourth attempt at the marathon, having got a little faster each year and still high on the surprise PB of the previous year.

Due to a family party our children were desperate to see their Irish cousins, and stayed with their grand-parents instead. This left us having a rare 'adults only' weekend, so we could partake of drinking and social-ising and Cloë could buy a last-minute ticket for the Ronan Keating concert next door to the hotel while I drank beer in the pub with running friends.

Saturday morning arrived, we were greeted with a biblical downpour, and all thoughts of a parkrun were binned in a favour of a lie-in.

Over the course of the day a combination of coinci-dences meant I found myself in the start pen for the 10k, having got a number only half an hour earlier. Running the first half comfortably, but at great pace, I entertained delusions of being the next Mo Farah – which were abruptly dashed on the return leg by a horrendous headwind. It then dawned on me how wind-assisted the out leg had been.

Come 7pm I was lined up for the 5k in a fancy dress outfit my loving wife had sorted at the last minute. Although the pace was relaxed the outfit made me sweat so much that I have new-found respect for anyone who runs a full marathon in an elaborate costume. Two races done in one day and after a convoluted journey, a spot for the half marathon was winging its way down from Milton Keynes. Maybe I could do all four?

After a hasty shower and a rushed dinner, a plan was made. As Cloë was running the half, I accompanied her to the start. Unfortunately, the early start meant we missed the hotel breakfast so I had only half a sausage roll and an Eccles cake to sustain me. Nonetheless, I felt relaxed and prepared, after all I was a professional at this marathon malarkey by now.

At 8am the half started. Conscious I had two hours before the marathon, I set off with a PB in mind, aiming for somewhere between 1h30m and 1h35m. The faster I finished the more time I'd have to get back for the marathon but also the more knackered I'd be for the next 26.2 miles. 1h40m would have been comfortable but would only leave 20 minutes to pass through the finishers section and run the intervening two miles to the marathon start.

Running largely 'to feel' I chipped along the course at a steady pace, hoping to hit the sweet spot between too tired to run and too late to make the start. On one of the switchbacks I passed Cloë running with a friend, Colin, looking very good and enjoying the event. Unlike me, they had no time constraints and were running just the one event.

As I write, she looks over my shoulder and reminds me that's because she's not a bloody idiot.

Crossing the line at 1h33m I barely broke stride as I thanked the always excellent volunteers for the medal and goodie bag, downed some water and set off on the run. Unsure of finding a taxi driver keen on taking a sweaty runner, and thinking it might be quicker to run, I resolved to keep it all under my own control. In my vanity I must admit that the appeal of doing the whole stupid stunt under my own steam appealed.

As the 'jog' to the start progressed and every road seemed to be uphill I began to doubt my choice. A taxi would have been easier. A wodge of notes was likely to have convinced any taxi driver on the relative profit for a two-mile journey even if he needed a few squirts of Febreze to remove the stench after he ejected me. The distance, by Google Maps, didn't seem to be dropping. At 10am I still couldn't see the park. Knowing the marathon course I'd elected to run for the start line, not the main entrance to the park as this was a lengthy walk/jog/sprint to the pens.

At 10.01 I started seeing hazard tape and marshals up ahead. How far into the course was this?

At 10.02 I started to hear cheering up ahead. How long would it take for all the pens to work through?

At 10.03 the lead bikes were coming towards me. How quickly do they pack up timing mats?

At 10.04 the lead runners passed me in the other direction. Hopefully the timing staff would be on double time for a Sunday and be working at a relaxed rate. Still wearing the race bid from the half I pulled it off and shoved it in my pocket, pulling out the marathon bib.

At 10.05 the main pack started to pass me. This might just work.

At 10.06 I was at the entrance to the park. How much further was the start mat? Was the pack of runners thinning out?

At 10.07 I could see the banners for the start. The gaps between the runners was getting bigger, looking more social than competitive runners.

At 10.08 I drew up to the start line, waved the marathon bib at the stewards, squeezed through the gap in the barrier for the elite runners (first time for everything) and joined the race just behind six blokes in a Viking longboat and Ben Smith from the 401 Challenge doing some media PR. He was about to start his 399th consecutive marathon and looked far fresher than I felt.

Jogging to keep ahead of the sweeper I swapped sweaty top for dry top and tried to pin the race bib on with as little loss of blood as possible. My stupid attempt to do all four races hadn't cost me a marathon. All I had to do was finish and that's easy, this was marathon 81 after all. What could possibly go wrong?

A lot. At the first aid station 3.5 miles in I was desperate for a drink. Rather than grab and run I detoured round the back, took a few bottles of water and downed them, followed by several more with High5 hydration tablets dropped in. I also dumped the goody bag with associated freebies from the half marathon in the bin. I shouldn't have been so thirsty so early in a race. My mind wandered back to the previous day and the realisation that I had mostly arsed about, drank beer and sweated my dehydrated arse off in a Chewbacca onesie for the 5k. Pace, so far, had been conservative but this was hard work. Also, the heat was getting to me.

Leaving the aid station, I grabbed discarded part empty bottles and dumped on my head. I was too hot, dehydrated and feeling hungry but I'm a pro. Leave my legs alone and they'll amble me around to 4hrs with no hassle. Of course.

Two miles out after the aid station I was struggling to maintain 10minute/mile pace, and I needed a wee. I never stop on marathons: wasted time. When the course met the half marathon route I'd completed just a couple of hours earlier, the difference in speed was considerable, but that's to be expected. Sadly, it got worse, and I could feel the bonk coming. Nothing specific felt wrong, just everything was hard. Like man flu but less fatal.

I stopped and queued at a toilet, ringing Cloë to see how she had got on. She answered in a panic assuming I was near dead, or why ring mid-marathon? Her race had gone well, and she snagged a PB with no issues from her previously broken ankle. I reassured her I wasn't dead and pushed on, desperate for the next water station and wishing my race would go as well as hers had.

In my befuddled state I was half a mile down the road before my brain pointed out the public toilets probably had water. Not the most hygienic but unlikely to kill me.

Over the next few miles I reduced to a run-walk. Two weeks previously I'd completed my first 50-mile race. It had been hard and required walking in sections. During these walk breaks, I had discovered how slowly I actually walk. Everyone passed me on the walks, but I slowly pulled them back on the runs and just about kept ahead until the next walk. It's a humbling experience to labour away with the fail bus chasing you down.

The one upside was that I rediscovered how friendly runners are. At my normal pace I've barely got the breath to talk, but now I could engage in great conversations as we repeatedly passed each other. Some of it was so choice it could even be described as 'banter'. We joked about our awful performance compared to expectations and how they'd likely be taking down the finishing arch before we got there. On each out and back we watched the sweeper bus behind and I realised that, in my arrogance, I'd not even considered the cut-off time. I hadn't needed to consider course cut-offs for the last 70+ marathons. Being timed out is something that happens to other people.

We reached the halfway point in 2h30m but the pace was descending to embarrassing levels and the walk breaks were getting longer. The weekend before, I'd led the local marathon from the start and didn't just finish well but managed my second ever outright win – admittedly in a small field and with limited competition. This weekend I was facing the prospect of being disqualified for lack of progress. The random conversations continued. Runners tend to open up to each other during a run in a way that you wouldn't normally with a stranger. One club runner from Norfolk described how his wife had sadly passed away just a few months previously. The simple act of getting out the door and lacing up his trainers for a run was helping him through the grief, and the marathon had been something to focus on that wasn't funeral plans, life insurance issues and the seemingly endless list of people needing to be informed of the end of his wife's life. Running for enjoyment, not that I was enjoying it much that day, seemed pathetic in comparison.

The upside of running (walking?) in the finishers' tee from the current year is the confused looks and shouts. One marshal declared me awesome for running two events (I didn't feel awesome, I felt like crap). Two runners in similarly oxygen-starved states debated for some time whether we were in 2017 and I was wearing last year's tee, or if it was still 2016.

Coming down the hill to the main pier I was overjoyed to see my clubmates and my supportive wife. She was shocked when I stopped for a chat rather than a fleeting kiss, although chat is probably not the best description for my moaning and whining. To shut me up she forced some of her kebab and chips in my face. Redway Runners clubmate Laura handed me a Pepsi which I downed and set back out towards Boscombe Pier, continuing my chats with a runner from Gosport Harriers as we swapped places over the next few miles.

The public were by now out in force, some spectating, some just enjoying ice cream and a walk in the autumn sun.

I could murder an ice cream about now, I thought. I've got cash. Do I have time to stop? Would I start again if I did?

Stopping for a kebab mid-marathon had been pretty embarrassing. Or genius. Either way it was quick as the food had been waiting. Standing in a queue of holiday-makers, stinking like a sweaty horse, patiently waiting to order a cone with a flake was probably a step too far so I averted my gaze from the ice cream van and pushed on.

I was relieved to reach Boscombe Pier. I had enjoyed running it during the 10k the day before and whipping along it on the half marathon earlier that day was exhilarating, but now it was just a big long bouncy wooden nuisance that eventually ended.

It was time to head back to Bournemouth Pier and the support crew. I passed another marshal who noticed the top and was incredulous that I'd run the half that morning. His brain visibly did the maths. 'How did this walking abomination cover 13 miles in two hours? How could he cover 13 miles at all when he looks a complete state?'

At Bournemouth Pier my salvation awaited, Cloë stood with a largely melted ice cream that I devoured in seconds. I'd made the right decision to avoid the ice cream van, both in terms of wasted time and pride as two ice creams in a single marathon would be shameful for someone that considers themselves a runner. With finest Cornish Cream dripping down my chin I lapped the pier (slightly less bouncy wooden nuisance) and meet Cloë again on the return leg to be handed an ice-cold Dr

Pepper. This was shaping up to be a race fuelled mostly on sugar and artificial ingredients.

Dropping off the pier I passed under the finish gantry at 17 miles. On the other side the finishers were going through and my watch confirmed that, last year, I'd have been with them. I hated last year's version of me, he was a smug idiot. This year I still had nine miles to go.

Walking the slow steady climb up to West Cliff past the hotel (if I had the car keys I could go home now...) I resolved to end the walking. The food and drink took effect and my legs remembered what they've been trained for. Two hundred miles a month for the last eight months had formed muscle memory. I started to keep a rhythm and pass some other runners.

This time I was not aiming for a PB but to salvage a finish under five hours and, with each passing mile, it was looking more likely. We dropped through a park onto the seafront and it was straight out and back. The miles were clocking down and getting easier, at a relative pace such that I could look ahead and plan my overtakes. I had become not just a runner again, but one of those annoyingly chipper runners having a second wind and weaving through the crowds, inadvertently reminding everyone else how slow they are. A few miles before I'd have sworn under my breath at this new version of me.

At 23 miles there is an uninteresting traffic island next to Poole Harbour. The significance is that it marks the home stretch. No longer does every step take you away from the finish line, it's now a step nearer. With a parkrun to go, it's the home straight. This helpful advice was met with grunts from the runners I passed. The pier doesn't appear to get any nearer and, if you're having a bad day, is a killer for motivation. With 23 miles in your legs the end is forever on the horizon but just out of reach, like the base of a rainbow, but with a medal and a sit-down more desirable than a pot of gold.

Fortunately, at my fourth Bournemouth, I was aware and ignored the pier. Two miles left. One mile left, I finally reached the home stretch and my cheering wife and clubmates again. One last turn by the pier and I went under the finish gantry for the fourth and final time that weekend.

It had been an amazing weekend of running and I'd answered the question that had been bugging me. It IS possible to run all four events. It's just not advisable. It also reminded me not to underestimate the marathon. I may well have, somehow, fallen into being an ultra-runner but I still needed fluids and fuel to get through any race.

Days later, some more experienced ultra-runners reminded me that I'd eaten heavily into my energy stores in the recent 50-mile event and my body had likely been living hand to mouth in terms of fuelling. When pushed hard with little sustenance there simply aren't the reserves to get through. If energy was cash I'd just attempted two lavish holidays in a row and the credit card had firmly said no. Time to start saving again!

Bournemouth Marathon Course Notes

Start – Not much around and a walk from bag lorries to start, so worthwhile wearing bin bag/old clothes to throw off at start, especially for the half marathon which starts at 8am.

The first half of the marathon has a lot of out and backs to see other runners and the elites.

There's two big(ish) uphill sections, which isn't a huge issue if you're expecting them. If you're from Milton Keynes, they are of Ben Nevis proportions. Don't kill yourself running up, better to power walk, and take the chance to drink/change iPod track or admire the views.

Fuelling – gels and water only, no sports drink. I prefer sports drinks, so I take some High 5 tablets with me to dissolve.

At mile 17 you do a lap of the main pier and then pass close to the finish gantry. You can almost touch it. Then you do a quick dogleg over the overpass and back down to the finish gantry again to really rub it in, before being sent up a climb away from adoring crowds to do a nine-mile out and back along the coast. If it's going well this isn't too bad. If you're struggling you dwell on the fact that every knackered step you take forward will need to be repeated back on even more knackered legs.

At mile 22 you take a turn inland, past annoying people relaxing in cafés and eating ice creams to loop a traffic island and then it's a straight run back. The final section it's best not to focus on the finish and the pier in the distance as it never seems to get any closer.

Mile markers are at times a little off due to placement of lamp posts and it's a fairly winding course. I normally get closer to 26.5m on Garmin so allow for that if you're going for a time.

Finally, I like to finish the race, run into sea, cramp up, fall over and nearly drown. It adds an element of danger.

19

BACK-TO-BACK MARATHONS

With a few marathons under the belt, you may get carried away and consider back-to-back marathons i.e. marathons on subsequent days. Daunting at first, especially if your typical post-race regime is two days on the sofa eating junk food and chocolate bars, but advantages include getting two steps closer to a 100 Marathon Club entry. They are also good endurance training, particularly if aiming for an ultra in the future.

Fortunately for me, Foxy's Enigma Running hold many small-scale marathon weekends in Milton Keynes, including the Quadzilla event, where certifiable idiots can part with good money to run laps of Caldecotte Lake and cover four marathon distances on four consecutive days. This is, of course, ludicrous and stupid. It would be even more stupid for a runner having just completed one marathon, and training for two in a week, to sign up for a Quadzilla event nearly a year in the future by which time he'd likely have gone off running altogether and taken up competitive eating competitions. So of course that's what I had done.

I first attempted the feat in 2013. I would recount the story but it is mostly a blur of discomfort. I finished each day having been passed by seemingly every runner. Importantly, I got my finishers' hoodie proudly proclaiming I had finished four marathons in four days, covering over 100 miles.

By chance I was wearing the hoodie at the leisure centre when taking the kids swimming some months later and was spotted by BBC Three Counties Radio hosts doing a live broadcast on fitness and well-being. With seconds to prepare, myself, Billy and Charlotte were live on air and explaining my passion for running. I tried my best to get across the benefits of running, the all-inclusive nature of the pastime, recount how I'd gone from fat bloke to slightly less fat bloke, and drop some subtle plugs for MK Lakeside Runners and Enigma Running. The star of the show was undoubtedly Billy who, at only four, recounted at length how Daddy 'wasn't very good at running and never won a race' and mostly 'sweats a lot and smells bad' at the end. Ribbed on the BBC by your own flesh and blood!

Despite the public humiliation I returned to the Quadzilla in 2015 and 2017 to expand my collection of finishers' hoodies. Enigma events have now become a staple of my marathon journey, and I know every inch of the Caldecotte Lake loop better than my own garden.

Foxy will likely name a wing of his mansion after me to commemorate my contribution to his mortgage.

Quadzilla 2017

Thursday, Quadzilla Day 1: This is my third entry to Quadzilla, and my game plan was to take it easy for first day. Now in its 7th year (2017), the event is organised by Enigma Running. Over the course of four days, competitors run marathons around Caldecotte Lake in Milton Keynes. Anyone managing to complete all four gets a hoodie. With most of the 60–70 participants attempting the full Quadzilla there is great support among the runners as each takes on their own personal challenge.

Whether you're a running god or a mere mortal, attempting four marathons is a big ask.

In single marathons you can finish in a fairly calorie-deprived and (mildly) dehydrated state and not be concerned since you have weeks, or months, to recover. With multi-day events you must always think about tomorrow, concentrating on drinking and eating while running and making sure you get the right recovery foods inside you afterwards. Despite being February, I still consumed at least 500ml of sports drink, 1l of water, an energy shot bottle and a small Coke every day.

My goal for day one was to avoid going off too quickly and suffering for the rest of the event. Although I felt strong, I held off racing anyone, finished in 3h40m in one of the most relaxed marathons I'd run in a long while. My right quad felt a little stiff though. Normally I would ignore this but, with three more races ahead, I broke the habit of a lifetime and tried to foam roller it.

If you've never tried a foam roller they look harmless,

like a large piece of packaging material. You lie or sit on it to use your body weight to roll out muscle tension or work on sore areas. Sounds almost relaxing? Sadly it hurts more than you could conceive and reduces even hardy runners to tears.

Friday, Quadzilla Day 2: On the second day it seemed that the foam roller of pain had not worked. I couldn't achieve a forward extension on my right leg and, after a while, my right calf joined in sympathy. Then the right hip added to the cacophony of complaint. This was very much a grin-and-bear-it day, the first time in a long while I'd had to battle to come in under four hours, hobbling over in 3h54m, not helped by a headwind on the exposed sections. At the start my target was 3h45–50m for all four days. That blew away on day two with accompanying doubts on keeping below four hours for subsequent days.

To focus on the important stuff, this was marathon number 90 and I was now in countdown mode to the 100th.

Saturday, Quadzilla Day 3: Like Bon Jovi I'm halfway there, but my right leg is living on a prayer. By luck, I tagged onto the Portuguese contingent who dragged me around at 8minute/mile pace to halfway. With brain disengaged I just followed them, ignoring the memories of a dodgy leg and the concern that I might be burning energy reserves I didn't have. Inevitably they lost me, but I had enough banked to allow steady pace to get home in 3h45m. This was nine minutes quicker than day two, maybe my leg would hold out after all.

Marathon 91 was done. One more left for my hoodie.

Sunday, Quadzilla Day 4: As we set off for day four the runners exclaimed more 'ooh arghs' than a field of Norfolk farmers. Legs seemed to be linked to mouth, bypassing the brain, and were objecting to another day of this nonsense. After some stuttering false starts we broadly set off 'running', ready for a final seven laps.

Initially, my legs were stiff, but they loosened and the first three laps went well. Halfway passed, I started to do the maths. The luxury of ten-minute miles would get me in at just over four hours but I wanted better, so pushed to gain on other runners on lap five. 3h45m looked possible, briefly, until my knee decided to make even the gentle slopes of Caldecotte hard work. Too much speed on the down sections meant it felt like it was struggling to hold my weight and in danger of buckling. After each aid station it took a few steps to get going again and flex enough to allow running.

Deciding I could afford to drop a few minutes and walk when needed, I dropped a few positions on the final lap but finished in 3h51m. With that, the final day of my third Quadzilla was done and dusted. I collected my hoodie and went home for a shower.

How to tackle multiple marathons

By intention or bad planning you may end up with marathons coming very close together.

Traditional marathoners often run a single marathon in the spring, maybe with a second in the autumn. With increasing interest in clubs such as Marathon Maniacs and the 100 Marathon Club it's not uncommon to undertake two in subsequent weekends or even subsequent days. Some advice on getting through these and avoiding mistakes follows.

- This is unlikely to be the route to PBs so you need to prepare mentally for two (or more) slower marathons rather than one all-or-nothing speed attempt.

- Pick which event you see as the main target. Focus on that. The other(s) will either be warm-ups or victory laps after. These are run for fun and completion rather than outright times.

- If on the first event you have an issue and know soon into the race you're not going to get the time you want, slow down. Enjoy it and save yourself for a second attempt later.

- As soon as you finish a marathon, you're preparing for the next. Drink a recovery drink, eat sensibly, rehydrate.

- Think about kit. Have a complete set of running gear for each marathon ready to go. Don't rely on washing your gear in between. Waking on Saturday morning to find your club top is still a sweaty ball in the bottom of the wash basket is not a great start, nor is finding that your only clean shorts are the ones with a hole in the pocket so all your gels fall out.

- If it's not on Strava it doesn't count. Get your watch back on charge and ready to go.

- If you can't run without music get your iPod on charge as well.

- Plan and ideally buy food and drink for all events. Don't assume you'll be able to buy that one flavour of sports drink that turns you into an unstoppable running machine when all you're passing on route to the next event is a dodgy off-licence.

- Plan travel and accommodation for all events. Two places may look close on a map but on Saturday afternoon with poor train service how are you getting 100 miles from the end point of one to the start of the other? Especially if you smell so bad no taxi will let you in.

- If they're on subsequent days (2in2, 4in4, 10in10) then treat the event like an ultra. You wouldn't pound up the hills on a 100-mile race so why do the same on day one of a four marathon series? Use the hills for a walk break, drink, eat. Chat to other runners. Ring your other half and reassure her/him you're not dead yet. Stick a selfie on Facebook to promote the fund-raising aspect of your midlife crisis.

20

MARATHONS 82 AND 96

Marathon 82 – Eton Dorney Marathon

Managed by two brothers, Steve and Jeff, *Running Miles* was founded to hold small, well-organised events around the Home Counties, this was their inaugural event and held at Eton Dorney Lake, venue for 2012 summer Olympics rowing competitions.

To kick-start interest they offered the event free and were, unsurprisingly, swamped. After hearing nothing for several months I had almost forgotten about it until a reminder email popped up a few weeks before. As it was only four days after Bournemouth, my initial plan was, assuming I had already run a decent time, to take the Eton Dorney event easy. After my silly running of all four races at Bournemouth I wasn't sure even if I'd manage to finish. Given that I can't say no to anything free I ignored the 50 miles taken out of my legs at the weekend and turned up for one of the best organised events I've partaken of.

Running Miles had hired an access road along the length of the lake, giving a handy 2.62 mile loop. With decent parking, a well-stocked aid tent and even porta-loos, it was a welcome sight. As we sipped our coffee, which made me realise that all marathons should start with coffee, they explained the route and the lap system.

If you've never run laps you should know that only large-scale events can afford chip timing. Most resort to manual counting. Typically, this is done by a volunteer sheltering in a marquee while marking runners off a list, hopefully avoiding said list being swept away by inclement weather. Some require runners to present a card for marking each lap, or issue them with elastic bands to drop every lap until the finish. *Running Miles* issued everyone with a plastic wristband, featuring tear-off tabs, one for each lap. It provided a great visual check and was a very professional approach. Later they changed this for tear-off Velcro tabs which are oddly satisfying to peel off as you run.

After the safety briefing we set off on the first of ten laps. With my legs feeling fresh I tucked in behind the leader for the first few before dropping into 3rd place.

The course is a simple out and back, and the road skirts the boating lake. It's scenic but exposed at times, and on the final few laps a headwind started to build on the out lap. The big advantage of out and backs is that runners pass each other multiple times, and a friendlier, social atmosphere is maintained. In some of the point-to-point, or long lap, events, runners can feel isolated and alone if there aren't many runners at their pace. As the race wore on it was satisfying to pull off the numbered tabs from the wristband. The race passed quickly in the knowledge that each completed lap meant a tenth of the race finished. The out and back also allows the runner to gauge relative performance and gaps. At each turna-round I could see the metronomic Steve Edwards closing me down with his seemingly effortless jog. As my pace dropped in the second half he caught and passed me.

Crossing the line and striking the finishers' gong I was amazed with a 3h24m and 4th place, my second quickest marathon for number 82. Four days previously I would have still had over nine miles left to run. Today I was putting my feet up and enjoying the view. The powers of recovery of the body can be truly surprising. After receiving a great bespoke medal, I was handed a goody bag and invited to fill it from the piles of drink and chocolate on offer.

Although the thought of food was far from my mind I knew the post-run hunger would hit on the drive home so I piled it high, making sure to include something for Cloë and the kids. Nothing says 'I love you' like free chocolate.

Marathon 96 – Milton Keynes 2017

It was all starting to get a bit real now. A hundred mara-thons had seemed an abstract concept for a number of years but now seemed very close.

My ambition for MK was to get a PB. It's a relatively

fast course and, being a dweller of milk'n'beans, I anticipated a lot of local support. I'd also been chosen as an ambassador for the event so had been blogging and generally promoting it on social media.

Training had gone well although trying to go faster and run longer for the 50 miler in April and 100 miler in June can be mutually exclusive. I maintained 200+ miles per month and enjoyed good speedwork sessions, so was miffed to miss a PB at the MK Rocket 5k (held the day before the marathon) by 2 seconds. That's fine, I thought, I'll save it for the marathon.

On the day of the event I unusually rocked up early for a photo call with the other ambassadors and met radio DJ Jo Whiley. I admit I was star-struck, having listened to her Evening Sessions shows with Steve Lamacq back in the 90s when I had hair and a marathon was still a chocolate bar.

As usual I missed the MK Lakeside Runners pre-race photo. Six years at MK Marathon and I always miss the photo as I'm in the toilet queue or someplace else.

After the customary McDonald's stodgy breakfast, and toilet stops, I wandered over to the start with the intention of sticking to the 3h15m pacer and getting a marginal PB (at the time, mine was 3h15m31s). I tend not to get a good result at MK as I try too hard, go out too fast and suffer to scrape in under 3h30m. This year the 3h30m pacer was world record holder Steve Edwards (who recently hit 800 marathons sub 3h30m!). He's a nice chap, but I sure as hell didn't want him to catch me.

We started off well, and Matt, the pacer, was bang on. Pace felt leisurely and, thanks to him, I ran the most even-paced, relaxed and consistent half marathon distance I've ever managed, with a time of 1h36m.

Then that voice in the back of my head reminded me that this was the point that I faded horribly last year. Wouldn't it be annoying if it happened again? A mile or so later it did. I'm not sure if it was the result of too many miles in training, a poor taper or a scumbag brain, although the early heat didn't help. From then it was a case of digging in and seeing what I could salvage.

Around Bancroft and Bradwell a lot of other runners pulled up with cramp. The early heat may have caught many out, but some sections were like a disaster movie with runners lying on the grass or convulsing against lamp posts, attempting to ride out the spasms. Pace-wise, they were likely aiming 3h15m–3h30m but their legs weren't co-operating. There's not a lot you can do at times like this except be glad it isn't you.

Skirting around Lodge Lake at mile 21, I was back to my usual nine times tables. Nine minutes per mile will see me over the 3h30m, eight will be under. When you intend to run at a steady 7:26minute/mile pace it's disappointing to be fleeting around 8:30.

I met some runners of a similar pace around mile 23 and we formed an impromptu pace group, pushing to keep ahead of the 3h30m pacer who was bearing down on us at the switchback on the college campus by mile 24. The ups and downs were proving hard on the pace, but we stuck together, each of us hoping that this was the last incline (as a local I knew it wasn't but thought best not to mention). I managed to save enough to do a decent impression of a fast finish and crossed in 3h27m.

It was my fastest of the year but 14 seconds slower than my previous MK and completing a pair of marginal disappointments for a year of hard training

Marathon 96 done, now to train for the 100 miler.

ACT 3

IF A MARATHON DOESN'T KILL YOU...

21

BEYOND MARATHON DISTANCE – ULTRAMARATHON

If you're reading this at the start of your running journey and planning for your first 10k or half marathon, the idea of running further than a marathon is, of course, ludicrous. That's because you haven't been let in on the secret of ultramarathons: walking and eating. While the marathon is a true test of perseverance in which every second counts and stopping to kiss a loved one could cost you a PB, an ultra is more about steady progress. And picnics.

Steady progress needs fuel. As you're likely running a lot slower, and walking the steep sections, you don't have to rely on sports drink and gels and can instead have the sort of food you would eat by choice. Typically ultras make the most of this, providing frequent aid stations groaning under the weight of sandwiches, sausage rolls, crisps, fruit fingers, pizza and sometimes hot food. Aside from the obvious taste advantages, it's also food that sits well enough in the stomach to sustain activity, alleviating concern about the gel wreaking its revenge.

Ultras are also less competitive than shorter distances. You're battling the distance, the course profile and often the weather. A few runners will be up at the front duking it out for trophies, but most are there to complete the challenge and are happy to work together, share food and keep company over stretches of the course, particularly during the night sections.

First Ultra – Making the Step Up

If you're considering taking the step up from marathon there are lots of options to choose from. Typically, the shortest are 30 miles or 50k, then through 50 miles, 100k/62 miles up to 100 miles and beyond.

As with your first marathon, you should be aware of cut-offs. These are often around 12–15hrs for 50 miles and 24–30hrs for 100 miles. If you're concerned about time limits, then a good interim choice would be an endurance event. These are anything from six to 24hrs and feature a lapped course; participants run as many laps as they can in the allotted time. If you can drag yourself around one lap, you're due the medal. It also provides a safe environment to attempt your target distance, never far from help or other runners. Thunder Run, Endure24, Equinox24 and others in the UK all follow this format and have solo, team or pairs entry.

My first 'mini' ultra was accidental when, due to a diary clash, I was unable to run a local marathon. Our ever-helpful Race Director, Foxy, advised he could move me to the 30 mile ultra the following day if I still wanted to run. This was a familiar course and just a further lap than usual, so worked well and went without issue physically, although there was a mental challenge in passing through marathon distance.

Bewl Water Ultra – 37.5 Miles

Bewl was my first attempt at a biggish ultra, although compared to the 100+ mile events it seemed barely worth the title. I'd been tempted to drop to the marathon distance in the preceding weeks but, following the advice of more experienced runners, I figured I might as well have a go.

My hopes of a fair club turnout for the event (with options of half, full and ultra) was set back by a clubmate's stag do the same day. There was more interest in rum than running. This left just one clubmate, James, and I to do the early morning trek to Kent and the Bewl Reservoir. We arrived just in time for me to register for the 8.30am ultra and join the other runners shivering in the morning chill. Doubting that I'd worn enough, I compared the other runners' clothing, which varied from tiny vests to full long-distance kit.

After a countdown we set off along the gravel path, rising to the lake. A previous winner had finished in 5h48m so I had hopes of placing highly. These were dashed when two runners stormed into the distance. I was in a chase group of 4–5 running around 7:30min/

mile pace, which was too quick for me to sustain. The lead pair dropped us without really trying.

We swapped places in our little group a few times until, after four miles, I decided to drop closer to my intended pace of around 8:45min/mile. By this time I had warmed up, and my buff had moved from ear protection to being worn around the wrist so I looked like a sweaty, low-rent freedom fighter.

The course mostly follows an unmade footpath around the lake, but also veers along small roads and past local houses. This arrived as relief from the rutted, tree-root-filled path until we faced the steep climbs of the country lanes – runnable for those doing the half, and not too much of a challenge for the full marathon runners, but for anyone foolish enough to attempt the full three laps they were daunting.

I elected to power walk and save my legs. This allowed a couple of runners to catch me, including one lady wearing so little clothing my goose bumps came out in sympathy.

At ten miles into the race I was around 9th place. We spread out, and the race became quite lonely for the first lap. Despite excellent route marking by Hermes Running, there were a couple of points where I started to doubt myself and was relieved when I saw marker tape ahead, confirming I hadn't misplaced myself in the countryside.

At 11 miles in, I couldn't help but think that, although I'd already run a fair distance, I still had over a marathon to go. Finishing the first lap around 1h40m, the marshals let me know I was in 8th place, which sounded better than the 9th I thought I was in, but made me wonder whether someone had dropped out already.

I knew the half marathon runners, including James, would have a ten-minute head start as I began the middle lap. With luck I might catch up with some of them. This proved to be the case and was a real boost for my enthusiasm. Most not only moved to one side to allow me to pass, but also cheered me on. Thinking back to my first few halves I can fully appreciate how inexplicable the choice to do nearly three times the distance would be to the less experienced runners. I tried not to ask myself exactly why I was doing this and what made me think I could complete it. The other runners' encouragement really helped me keep going. Eventually I passed some of the slower marathon runners who'd started an hour after me and that, too, helped mentally.

I lost a position to a friendly runner who caught me in the woods sections. He'd done a practice lap of the course on a previous weekend, and I didn't feel too badly about losing to someone who'd clearly put extra effort in. Fortunately, a few miles later I caught another runner and regained 8th place.

The second lap's pace was very controlled. I walked the hills, took on water whenever I could and enjoyed the most relaxed long run I'd ever done. Beginning to see the appeal of ultra-running, I skipped through the fields eating handfuls of chocolate brownie or flapjack. Coming to the end of the second lap I realised the water bladder in my Camelbak rucksack was empty and, with only one lap to go, elected to drop it by the finish line and run with just a hand bottle.

The aid station was congested with runners, but I

noticed I was next to the female ultra-runner who had passed me a lap earlier. I'd slowed a lot in the intervening 14 miles but she'd evidently fared worse. We chatted briefly on the climb to the reservoir before I pushed on, slipping up to 7th.

Passing marathon distance around 3h55m I was shocked by how well I felt. I'd covered the 26.2 miles over an hour quicker than my first marathon yet felt relatively fresh. The remaining miles were a mental fight between the pessimistic and optimistic sides of my mind.

Eleven miles to go! That's less than a normal Thursday run. It's nearly a half marathon though, and those miles hurt.

Nine miles now. That's a typical Wednesday 5am run in the woods. Yes, normally following a good night's sleep.

With 30 miles done, there are only 7.5 left to go, that's *nothing*.

Thirty-one miles was the furthest I'd ever run in one day. Not only was every extra step self-discovery and a distance PB, but also another agonising step into the unknown.

While walking (probably more like ambling) up one of the final hills I was caught and passed by a female runner. Assuming she was a marathon runner I took little notice until, out the corner of my eye, I spotted her green bib colour denoting ultra-distance.

I'd lost a place. This gave me enough of a kick to start running again and I began to reel her in, pushing as hard as my little legs would allow.

I was barely averaging 10min/mile pace by now so 'fast' was very relative. Passing sloths would have been unimpressed by my relative speed as I inched past, like two lorries fighting for position on an uphill motorway. I finally regained position and determined not to lose 7th again. I just had to slog out the remaining 10k – 'only' 10k, but it felt like a long way to go. Finding the energy from somewhere to check over my shoulder, I found I was almost imperceptibly opening the gap. I was also gaining on some runners ahead.

Finally, in a small group of marathon runners, I left the trail and arrived at the visitor centre for the lap of the car park. The marathoners spurred me on and I managed to turn my legs over a little faster, pulling away from them and keeping my ultra competitor at bay. Making the most of the downhills I pushed on to the finish, crossing with a respectable sprint and a total time of 5h50m, an average pace of 9:15min/mile. This was quicker than my intended average, achieved more by excessive early speed than steady pacing. The race was won in an impressive 4h53, nearly an hour off the previous winning time.

James was waiting for me in the finish tent with two cold beers and, much to the amusement of the other runners, we toasted our success before climbing up the hill to the car.

My first ultra had been everything from relaxed to agonising. Now we needed to get back to Milton Keynes and rehydrate at our clubmate's stag do. Judging by the drunken text messages we'd received there was a fair bit of catching up to do.

22

TEAM RELAYS: ENDURE24 – JUNE 2016

My first attempt at an ultra-relay event was unplanned. Lying on Galé beach in Albufeira, recovering from a nail-biting beach football game with my son (narrowly losing 24 goals to 25) and bemoaning my pitifully low recent mileage, I heard my phone beep. It was an invitation from Redway Runners running mate Jen. Could I take a spot on a five-person mixed team in ten days' time at Endure24? One of the runners had dropped out and the remaining members were searching for idiots willing to camp and run for a weekend.

I was unsure how many idiots had declined before I was asked.

As luck would have it, Cloë had other plans that weekend and in any case felt no keen desire to sleep under canvas, having been mentally scarred by camping trips as a Brownie. The children had been bugging us to go camping for years, so accepting would let them experience the fun of a British summer in a leaking tent while Daddy tried to run off too many tapas and countless jugs of sangria. All I needed to sort out was sleeping bags, a tent, groundsheet and, doubtless, a raft of other camping items I didn't yet know of.

As with similar events, Endure24 allows runners to compete in a relay to run as many laps of a set loop as possible within 24 hours. Categories are based on mixed or single-sex teams and overall size, with solo or pair options for the exceptionally keen. With a combination of running, camping and drinking it's a festival for runners: Le Mans 24hr for foot power.

One Saturday morning, in a car groaning with borrowed equipment, we arrived at a slightly muddy field just outside Reading. The rest of the team (Jen, Julie, Stuart and Dennis) had arrived on Friday and set up base camp. Cloë and I had entered for the local Marston Forest 5k that night, with both children to run the fun run, hence the late arrival.

After finding my team, there was just the simple matter of erecting a tent I'd never seen before, with no clear idea what overall shape it should be. After a few false starts we got it set up while mine and Jen's kids ran around having a great time and competing to see who could sustain the worst injury from a Nerf dart.

Wandering to the start, Julie got ready for the first of the five-mile laps while we staked out spots to watch the runners come through, led by an ex-army tank, chased down by the speedy runners and one glory hunter who ducked past the tank and ran in front, goofing it up for the crowd. The 24 hours starts at noon Saturday and final laps must begin before noon Sunday, allowing closer to 25 hours depending on speed of the final lap. Based on success in previous years my team had agreed to rotate by completing a lap each, including through the night to keep the running intervals shorter and hopefully faster, but sacrificing the longer rest periods that double laps would have offered.

Lacking experience, I accepted advice from the experts.

Second on the roster, I changed into running gear and waited in the changeover area, trying to remember what top Julie was wearing so I'd recognise her as she approached. The first changeover is very congested as most runners complete within a short window. Add nerves and excitement, and you have a large crush of people leaning over barriers, trying to distinguish which of the Lycra-clad lunatics approaching is theirs.

Julie appeared, wearing an entirely different top to what I remembered her in. This didn't bode well for future handovers if I couldn't even recognise a club-mate when fresh and awake. Fortunately, she was less pathetic and picked me out of the crowd to hand over the electronic wristband, and I was off on the first of an expected seven laps.

The course follows a tarmac road before changing to a stone track as it continues up a hill, a long gentle climb that takes its toll on not-so-fresh legs that thought they were done for the day. Being quite exposed, it is probably the worst section of the route.

Eventually, the track enters the woods to wind and climb its way across the local terrain. The first half of the course was wide enough for easy passing and runners encouraged each other, especially up the infamous Heartbreak Hill which magically grows every lap to Everest-like proportions and attacks your calves. The course then narrows and becomes more of a traditional mud and packed soil trail which is the best section. Diving past other competitors and jumping across ditches makes runners concentrate on the task at hand and not dwell on how many laps are left.

Breaking through the trees for the final grass section before the handover, I was drenched in sweat having pushed relatively hard. Passing other runners, and relieved that the previous night's race hadn't taken too much out of my legs, I looked for Jen in the mass huddle of runners at changeover.

The downside of diminutive teammates is that they're very hard to find in a crowd. I passed over the band and watched her disappear into the stream of runners. My lap had been challenging and varied, but it was now time for three hours' rest and the opportunity to introduce the children to the wonders of chemical toilets and outside water taps.

The weather stayed dry and we outperformed the planned 45-minute laps, gradually creeping ahead of schedule. This was great for the leader board but shortened the rests. To ensure we were in place ready for the handover, the breaks were closer to two and a half hours, which was not something to look forward to overnight. Five fast miles was enough to ensure we were drenched in sweat by the end and needing a complete change of clothes. I started to wonder if I'd packed enough kit.

Come 10pm I was waiting at handover with head torch, and a hand torch as backup, ready to start my fourth lap, my first in the dark. The children were fast asleep in the tent, snoring peacefully on airbeds, and it felt odd to have been part of a race for ten hours but still to have only run a half marathon distance. My laps had been consistent, but I wondered how the night run would go.

The pen of runners peered through a floodlit arch into the gloom, trying to pick out their teammates. What was difficult in the daytime became almost impossible at night as a sea of head torches dazzled us as the runners came past. Starting to wish we'd worn fairy lights or similar for identification I finally saw Julie, made the handover and set off up the hill. The first section's bushes were decked with glow sticks and looked magical.

As soon as we entered the woods our head torches were tested. What is fine for running through your local town with street lights and passing cars seems pathetic in pitch darkness when potholes and tree roots jump out at you. Most runners seemed to slow, but I was keen to keep the pace up and confident that I could remember the main hazards. I elected to push on while hoping I didn't end up eating mud.

As the path narrowed, I used the hand torch as well for supplementary lighting. It was a cheap LED unit and only just sufficient for picking out the route. At a couple of points, the path in front was illuminated like Wembley Stadium as faster runners with superior lighting came past. If they hadn't been so fast I'd have asked them for recommendations for next year, their units were simply in another league.

The VW Campervan positioned at the bottom of Heartbreak Hill came alive at night and was banging out Jimi Hendrix and pulsing with neon as I approached. I thank Jimi for keeping me going up that hill. Where the route narrowed and weaved through the trees, the event crews had decorated the trunks with fairy lights. Charging towards the finish, it was awesome to experience the confusion and difficultly of a night-time changeover. Some other runners reported seeing fairies in the woods; this may have been arranged by the event staff or were possibly the result of sleep deprivation and excessive alcohol.

Back at the camp I gasped for a drink in the warm night air, and downed a cider for essential carbs while peeling off my soaking top and pinning my race number to the next. Although I really needed a shower, the queue was long and I felt that sleep would be more beneficial. I settled for a standing wash from the outside tap, pulled my onesie on and lay in the tent, hopeful for as much of the two to three hours sleep I could get. My gear was prepared for the next lap and, like many people in the campsite, I lay still on a slowly deflating air bed, willing sleep to come.

All too soon Dennis knocked on the tent. He'd returned from his lap and Julie had started, so this was a 35-minute warning before lap five. Tired and yawning like a bear waking from hibernation I stumbled over with my better head torch on, wrapped in a blanket for warmth.

The changeover is an odd place in the middle of the night. The competitive teams were still desperate to perform quick handovers, sprinting onto the course through groups of sleepwalking zombies. I was ahead of schedule so wandered to the tent to watch the results update onscreen. They made little sense in my addled state so I returned to the barrier hoping not to swallow a passing runner with a world-record breaking yawn.

I almost missed Julie but she suddenly burst into view, taking my blanket and sending me off for lap five. It was 1.40am and any sensible person would be asleep. With the decent head torch, I was able to really push through the dark section, avoiding being overtaken at all. This felt like an achievement.

By this time the solo runners were over halfway and going strong. Most wore banners or had messages written on their bodies to identify them, and all of us made a point of encouraging them on. I like to think we did help in some small way.

Night laps are a strange experience and play with your sense of pace. I was chipping along with another runner, both of us refusing to back down, when I noticed my pace had crept to 6:20min/miles – far too quick for a half marathon, never mind an ultra. On other occasions you work your legs hard to be rewarded with mile splits as if you were walking.

With this many laps done, I had the course memorised and looked ahead to the fun sections, counting down to the home stretch and the handover. My previous rest strategy had worked well so, after that lap, I refuelled with another cider, washed under the tap and lay down to rest.

The next knock on the tent flap really was too early

as Stuart had experienced an issue with his knee and pulled out. This left just four of us and reduced the rest gaps even more. It was already light at 4am, so I binned the head torch and carried the hand torch to satisfy the rules (one torch per runner from 8pm to 6am). This was lap six and I made a very uncharacteristic mistake, forgetting to start my Garmin! Coming up to the 2k mark I looked down to check my progress and saw a blank distance and pace. I was genuinely torn between running back to restart and go again, or plodding on. My teammates might throttle me if I added an extra 4k loop back to my turn, so I decided to suppress my anguish at having run and not logged it.

I'll likely need counselling at a later date, but it encouraged me on as punishment for my stupidity.

At the bottom of Heartbreak Hill (again) one runner heard me coming and stepped to the side. I thanked him for his consideration, but he then bellowed up the hill: 'fast runner coming, everyone keep to the side!' With an audience expecting someone fast, I had no choice but to adjust my lopsided wobble into something that might be called running. Trying to breathe less like an asthmatic pig, I did my level best to live up to the billing. I've never been so grateful to reach the top and be out of sight so I could recover before the final push to finish lap six.

Getting back to the camp just before 5am I slipped into the tent, changed back into the onesie and was dozing when the children woke, unbelievably excited to have spent their first night camping. I couldn't resist messaging Cloë to let her know she might have got out of their first camping trip but there may well be others.

She was exactly as excited as I had known she wouldn't be.

The kids had both slept well and refused to go back to sleep as they were looking forward to a bacon and marshmallow breakfast. With the addition of bread and ketchup, most of the food groups were represented. We had coffee, hot chocolate and orange juice as a warm-up before heading out for lap seven where I was dragged around by the prospect of bacon and, despite tired legs, only marginally slower than on previous laps. Jen's husband Andy was on incineration duties and got the disposable barbeques going, 'assisted' by four excited children.

I jogged back to camp with a hunger for burnt pig. We cooked up far more bacon and sausages than we could eat, before cracking out the marshmallows. This was one of the best bits of the weekend, according to my children.

Then it was time to pack and get ready for our bonus laps. The plan had been to run seven laps each, but a combination of a better pace and reduced numbers made it look like we'd all get an extra lap in. Just after 10am I stood waiting for Julie to complete the first of the unforeseen laps. I expected to run around 40 minutes for my lap and similar from Jen so, with luck, we should be back in time for Dennis to start before the 12 noon cut-off. All would depend on how much the extra mileage had caused us to fade. Julie appeared under the arch at 10.26 and it looked like we'd manage it. Taking the band for the final time I ran out of the pen, uttering a few choice words as my legs initially refused to work.

234

The fools had thought they were done with running for the day!

Making a special effort to thank all the marshals on my final lap I was back in just over 41 minutes, passing duties to Jen who, after a very comfortable 40 minutes, handed over to Dennis. My running was done for the weekend, having covered eight laps and 40 miles.

From just after 12.00 the teams made their way back to the start, and it was great to see everyone complete the final few hundred metres with the last runner of each team. While waiting for Dennis, so we could do the same, we became aware of excitement in front of us as a chap called Matt went down on one knee to propose to his girlfriend Amy as she crossed the line. She accepted in the middle of a crowd of sweaty runners all clapping and cheering.

Wearing our event tees (mine was overly snug as I had replaced a slender lady in the original team and looked like Daffyd Thomas from Little Britain) we grabbed Dennis as he approached and crossed the line together. It was the perfect end to a great impromptu weekend away. We'd covered 36 laps between us and came 7th in the mixed category of around 120 teams.

For anyone seeking to join the 100 Marathon Club it's worth noting that relay events don't meet their qualification standards. If you run the event solo, it would count assuming you completed marathon distance. Some take objection to this exclusion arguing they've run over the 26.2 miles in a single event but, to my mind, the gaps almost make it a series of five-mile races with cider and bacon stops. Some stops at ultras can be long, but I essentially ran for 40 minutes, spent three hours eating, drinking and having Nerf gun fights and then another 40-minute run. Plus, I didn't get the cliff edge collapse of pace that typifies any of my marathons so to my mind it can't have been one.

My top tip for first-timers would be to use a running number belt as swapping race number between tops was a hassle and reduced valuable sleep time. I'd also suggest a gazebo or similar as rain made it unpleasant to sit out while it was still too hot in the tents. Short laps mean you can avoid gels and sports products, and stick to eating real food. The location of your camp is worth considering at these events as you'll be making frequent trips to the toilet, catering and start line, so something central is good.

23

STEPPING UP AGAIN

Having knocked off 40 miles in 24 hours at Endure24 and been witness to the awful gurning faces of the solo runners, I felt intrigued to sample their indescribable pain of achievement. I started looking for longer races. Running chum Jen persuaded me to join her on the Centurion Running 50 mile event, South Downs Way 50 (SDW50), the following year. I think I mentioned earlier that she was a bad influence.

I had also put my name on the waiting list for the Chiltern Wonderland (CW50) in the prior September and promptly forgotten all about it. Come August I received a message telling me that I'd reached the top of the list and had a week to accept a vacated spot. After discussion with Cloë I signed up and vaguely wondered about doing some training.

Preparation for a 50 miler

Unlike shorter events, ultras from 50 miles up tend to have mandatory kit lists. These vary with length, location and likely weather but, as a minimum, tend to include a litre of fluid, head torch, emergency whistle, survival blanket and a waterproof jacket, sometimes trousers as well.

The last two are where you start to learn you know nothing about what waterproof means. Most running jackets aren't technically waterproof and are more often stated as windproof. As a minimum the mandatory waterproof jackets are 10,000mm hydrostatic head. This may sound like Greek or even Geek, but is simply a measure of how much water the fabric can withstand when tested. 10,000mm means the fabric didn't allow water through when tested underneath a ten-metre tube filled with water. Where this is coupled with taped seams, meaning all joints in fabric have a permanent impermeable tape attached from within, you have a waterproof jacket that won't allow rain in and will pass kit check.

The downside is cost. You can easily spend over £200 on this kind of jacket, so it's worth shopping around. Cotswold Outdoors, Go Outdoors, Tog 24 and Millets all have items that fit the bill.

With just over a month to go, I decided to do a long run wearing the hydration vest (a posh version of a ruck-sack, now favoured for ultras) packed with all the gear. I chose a nine-mile section of the nearby Greensands Ridge: starting in Woburn, cutting across the abbey grounds and ending by Millbrook car proving ground near Bedford. This promised to be an easy navigation route with few made roads or paths.

Throwing a few gels and energy tablets into my new vest pockets I set off. The route is beautiful, and I ran with deer, pheasant and muntjac. We were setting off in the evening, but conditions were hotter than expected and the litre of water was used up quickly. At Millbrook I felt a big drop in energy and took one of the gels, adding an energy tablet to my remaining water.

Six miles from home it got dark and I had to pull out the head torch I'd carried just for the weight, but was now glad I had included. I drank my remaining water rapidly and refilled thankfully at a tap outside Woburn Abbey.

Getting back to the car after covering just under 20 miles I knew that I had learnt a lot from the run. A litre of water was insufficient for 20 miles. I needed more food, having properly bonked on the way back. Wooded sections are a lot darker in early dusk than you appreciate and, despite a warm evening, my sodden top and a gentle wind had cooled me considerably. I could have done with a dry top to swap into. My running vest, a cheap own-brand item from Decathlon was good enough. Some of the pockets weren't as easy to reach as the more expensive brands doubtless were but, overall, I was pleased with it and had finalised what I'd be carrying for the CW50.

Final Preparation for the Chiltern Wonderland 50

By the final Thursday before my first 50 miler, my normally relaxed approach to running had started to fade. Having a mandatory kit list makes your approach a bit more serious. My race vest had been packed for over a week and I'd run several practice routes wearing the intended kit. It was the end of summer, the weather had been great and the ground was dry. Practice runs on trails had been done with a recently broken-in pair of Adidas road shoes with a lightly lugged tread. They too had been perfect.

The week before the race we got some awful rain, and a few on the event Facebook group popped out to test the route, and recommended trail shoes. I was now in limbo between tackling the race with proven shoes, that might not have the needed grip, or switching to trail shoes with less cushioning and which I'd not worn over ten miles. Argh!

It wasn't helped by it being a single-lap course so, whatever choice I made, I would have to live with it for many, many hours. Some 50 mile events are either lapped or allow drop bags at aid stations, so give you a chance to change shoes if needed.

At this stage I had no real plan for pacing. Having previously covered 38 miles in under six hours, part of me thought: 'just' another 12 miles would be achievable in another two hours, three at the outside, bringing me home in eight or nine hours. This prediction was roundly dismissed by more experienced ultra-runners, whose advice ranged from marathon time x2.5 for a 50 miler on similar terrain, to assuming a second 25 miles would take twice the time. The result of all this is that not only did I not know what shoes to wear, I didn't know how fast to go.

In an attempt to calm my nerves, I'd printed up a small table with the checkpoints, the distance, presence of toilets and expected time based on a steady 11min/mile pace. As a backup, it also included 12min/mile pace and the dreaded cut-off times.

The big marathons have a cut-off and often a sweeper bus moving at the equivalent pace to time people out. The bus will hit halfway at three hours for a six-hour cut-off, and anyone caught will be asked to either board the 'fail' bus or continue on the pavement so the road can be re-opened to traffic. The advantage of this is you can see the sweeper approaching and if you stay in front, even if only by feet, you're still in the race.

On trail events, each checkpoint will typically have a cut-off time for safety. Ideally, you'll reach each checkpoint well ahead and never be troubled. If you get lost, or have a low period, you might be forced to stop at a checkpoint. No one wants to be listed a DNF (Did Not Finish). Without a physical sweeper you may not know you've fallen off pace and have timed out. Particularly at a first event, you might be taking it steady, saving energy for the later stages and get timed out unintentionally.

Do check the event website for the published cut-offs and distances. Knowing distance between checkpoints will also help you plan fuelling strategies. For those keen to avoid pooping in the woods, toilet facilities can be marked as well.

Depending on length of the ultra, remoteness and frequency of aid stations, some events allow your crew to meet you at designated points. Crew is probably a rather grand name to bestow on your wife/husband/mate standing in a field holding a bottle and a dry top. If your race is going well they'll likely receive a sweaty hug and a rain-soaked top as reward for standing in the arse end of nowhere for three hours making small talk and wondering if they have time to go pee behind a tree. If you're in bits they have the unenviable task of trying to lash you back together, emotionally or physically, to keep going. If they're really lucky, they'll get to pop your blisters, cover them with plasters and go vomit in a bush after the dirtiest task they've ever undertaken.

More problematic for the crew and the volunteers at aid points is being the voice of reason. Runners will likely want to quit at times so may well need some encouragement or outright mockery to get their head back into the run: 'You didn't come this far to quit now, did you?' Or, 'Are you going to give up and waste all those training runs because your foot hurts?' Alternatively, it may be more serious and their job will be to encourage runners to see sense and stop. Those training runs really were for nothing after all.

Some ultras allow, or even have a mandatory requirement of a pacer for some or all of the race, typically the later or overnight stages. A pacer is another grand name for a friend willing and able to accompany you and offer encouragement in the form of compliments or remind you to grow a pair, pull up your big girl/boy pants and get moving, depending on your personal preference for carrot or stick. They can also assume responsibility for following the route, reminding the runner to drink, eat and wee and helping them add layers during the night. For longer events, or if you're particularly pushing the pace, you may need several pacers, swapping at aid stations to ensure legs fresh enough to maintain your record setting pace. We can but dream.

Pacing someone is good practice before undertaking your own ultra, but also a stressful experience. Messing up your own race is one thing, leading your exhausted friend six miles off course and jeopardising their months of training is something else.

For CW50 the organisers, Centurion Running, published cut-off and expected leaders' times. Putting these in a table allows you to see the best and worst-case scenarios and identify the harder sections of the course. In the case of CW50, the paces are similar as the course profile is the same throughout with no extended climbs. It gains 5,600ft or 1,700m in elevation over the course. The leaders will cover 50 miles at a quicker pace than my (and probably your) half marathon.

The other purpose of the table is that, when your brain has turned to mush and you want to end it all, you can check the distance to the next aid station and, hopefully, realise that walking isn't going to end your race.

The cut-off time of 13 hours sounds very easy when you calculate to over 15-minute miles. That's basically a purposeful walk and could well be twice your average marathon pace so it's easy. Right? Except it's double the distance, up and down hills, and through cattle gates and over stiles. With a solid 13 hours of walking you need to allow for aid stations and potential diversions. Only the most dedicated employee would be on their feet for 13 hours without a coffee break.

Race Day – Chiltern Wonderland 50

On Saturday morning on the way back to Goring Village Hall, I shared a lift with two internet strangers, Helen and Stuart, who, much to the disappointment/relief of Cloë, were lovely and also made no attempt to harvest my organs. Last-minute indecision between road shoes and trail shoes was settled by my leaving the trail shoes at the front door where I definitely would have seen them in the morning and certainly wouldn't have been able to walk past without noticing.

Kit inspection was efficient and organised, and within minutes of entering the hall we had numbers pinned and were ready to go. With my drop bag stowed and most pre-race toilet stops complete, there was little left to do but wait. My initial plan of completing in eight hours had been adjusted by the Facebook group so, packed in one of the pockets, were timings for 11- and 12-minute pace, as well as the cut-off times in case it all went horribly wrong. I'd been warned the elevation gain was serious. Living in Milton Keynes makes most of these figures meaningless as hills are something that happen to other people.

Walking to the start after the race briefing I loaded up the course on my Garmin. In the unlikely event that the almost excessive course marking wasn't enough, technology had my back.

The claxon sounded and we started on a slow and steady pace along the river bank. After 70 marathons I knew that I still set off too fast, so started towards the rear to adjust. My plan for the first half was to 'hold back' and likely 'hold on' for the later stages. As the crowd thinned I looked down at my watch. Garmin confirmed I'd been running for nearly ten minutes and covered two feet. It appeared I had no idea how course function worked and my super long battery life Garmin was now as much use as a £5 stopwatch from the market. Fearful of restarting my watch and losing overall elapsed time, I vaguely hoped it might still be recording in the background, so left it alone and started tracking on my backup Garmin.

The first section of the course is best described as undulating but, aside from the odd cattle gate and one hill, easily runnable. A good pace can be maintained. A few stiles crop up as you approach the first aid station, Tokers Green at ten miles. Centurion running allows 2h40 to make it this far and I was well under. After a quick top-up of fluids and the first of many, many Cokes I set off with 40 miles to go. It was further than I'd ever run before.

Thinking I'd best check the distance to the next station the volunteer finished my sentence for me and confirmed only 7.7 miles further. Not only do they tend to you, they read your mind.

Stage two is more of the same in terms of terrain and scenery. When able, I made a deliberate effort to take in the wonder of the British countryside and the feeling of being miles from anywhere while still so close to London. The stiles were becoming more regular but, after the umpteenth cattle gate, I wished they were of a more consistent design as I flailed at yet another variation of lock mechanism.

The second aid station was on Bix Common and, in my haste, I nearly ran past before noticing. After more Coke and a tentative few sandwiches and crisps I was off again.

Having been warned by more experienced runners how much time you can lose at checkpoints and how hard it is to restart if you sit down, I'd elected to grab the food and eat on the hoof.

The section between Bix and Ibstone is where the bigger climbs start, with two in particular taking the breath away with both the views and the effort. A final climb out of the sleepy village of Turville towards Cobstone Windmill was especially steep for a flatlander like me, and my ambling climb with sausage roll in hand was caught by the race photographers from their sniper-like position on the hill.

Fun fact: Turville was the filming location for the TV series, *Vicar of Dibley*.

These climbs exposed just how much I lack walking speed. Being mainly a marathon runner, walking is something I only ever do to chat to supporters or find a bin for the gel that's been making an unpleasant re-appearance. It's much more integral to the ultra and I have only one speed: really slow, like a man enjoying a leisurely lap of the local park in his lunch break. Other walkers passed me with no great effort, managing a much better return on their investment of energy. I didn't realise it initially, but I'd spend the rest of the race switching positions with the same few people as any gain made on my runs was eaten into and reversed during their walks.

By the next checkpoint at Ibstone I'd covered just over half the distance. Chugging more Coke and some orange segments that seemed like fruit of the gods, I overheard one of the marshals talking a runner into carrying on. Each was insistent that making it to the next aid station was inevitable/impossible and neither seemed keen on changing their mind. The cut-off at this point is a generous 6h40 so the confidence-stricken runner had nearly two hours to be convinced to push on. The marshal was keen to make the most of it, having no doubt seen countless in similar predicaments and knowing which choice will see you awake the next day broken but triumphant, or just broken.

Leaving the checkpoint to cross some fields and into woods, I had my first course issue. Somehow missing the obvious markings, I set off on what felt like the right route only to have my watch beep alarmingly as I strayed further into the woods. It was more than the glorified stopwatch I thought, and I retraced my steps to the massive and 'completely impossible to miss' course markings.

The section between Ibstone and Swyncombe has the two biggest hills on the course in a relatively short nine-mile section. Once again, I was passed on the climbs but made back distance on the running sections. I was slightly hampered by my feet slipping in my shoes and banging on the toe boxes on downhills. It was painful but my mind was taken off it as I entered a race of epic proportions on one of the short flat sections.

Another runner approached, breathing lightly and seemingly bouncing along the ground. Every man and his dog were passing me walking. I resolved not to let this happen during the runs and lengthened my stride, attempting the closest to a fast run I could. He was still gaining! Maybe this was the temporarily paused runner from Ibstone? The pep talk had done him well, the rest had worked, and he was cracking through the field.

As he drew level I looked across to confirm. No one there. I looked down and saw a boy of maybe nine out for a run with his dad on a Saturday afternoon, effortlessly chipping along at a pace neither I nor his dad (dwindling in the background) had a chance of matching. I was relieved to slow as our routes parted.

After the aid station at Swyncombe I was getting into the swing of the stops with my race vest off and bladder open with fresh tablets in when I reached the table. The helpful staff had it filled before I could even ask. I stopped to re-tie my shoes before grabbing a handful of the jam wraps which had now replaced orange segments as the best food stuff on Earth. Shortly after leaving the aid station the course takes a cut through the local church and I nearly missed it in my eagerness to stuff fuel down my face.

Swyncombe to Grims Ditch undulates but most climbs are short with very fast runnable downhill sections, perfectly inclined to aid a decent prolonged pace without being too steep for tired legs. A gentle climb follows, up through a farm to the final aid station positioned in a turn-off from the road.

More jam wraps and Coke, and the final section

starts. I had 41 miles done with the cut-off to this point at 10h40. Being nearly three hours ahead with the best part of five hours to cover just nine miles took my mind off the fact that this was three miles further than I'd run before and yet again I was venturing into the unknown. Maybe my legs would stop complaining and part company with me at 45 miles?

Just before my backup watch died, somewhere around 42 miles, I felt that I was on target for just outside of ten hours, well within my target. Coming under ten hours seemed like a stretch but achievable, although my hungry and tired brain couldn't calculate distances to any more accuracy than 'between five and six miles'. Attempting to get my main watch working I'd lost the elapsed time, so had only a vague idea of distance and was reduced to judging the time by the dwindling evening sun. What a bloody amateur.

Not long after my failed feat of mental arithmetic a runner surged past and I recognised him as the 'nearly DNF' from 20 miles previously. Whatever the marshal had said had done the job. He shot past like a scalded cat.

Two biggish climbs were ahead at 43 and 45 miles but they seemed achievable. These hills are lonely and unremarkable in the local landscape. If they could be picked up and plonked in Milton Keynes they'd be alive with runners and cyclists eager for hill reps.

With what felt like three miles left I passed a smiling volunteer with a cow bell, enthusiastically ringing away. I was sure it was the lady from earlier in the run, but she seemed like a memory from the distant past when my legs worked and climbing over stiles didn't elicit a torrent of swear words.

She cheerfully informed me that this was the final section and it was 'mostly' downhill from here. I forced down my one remaining energy shock block and set off into woods for the run back into Goring. With my legs loosening up I was something between disappointed and relieved that I'd have no record of a final few miles that felt like a blistering pace and not the zombie death walk they probably were. Coming into Goring I caught another runner and together we passed seemingly every pub as a final cruel punishment. While keen to finish I would happily punch a nun for a pint about then. Reaching the village hall, I still hadn't caught the runner in front but he had unwittingly pulled me through the town. I clocked in under the ten hours.

Inside the village hall, the volunteers were brilliant. I was almost bodily lifted from finish table, medal collection, and photography, through to tee shirt collection. They even retrieved my drop bag to save my tired legs. Short of a massage and an offer of a lift home I'm not sure that they could have done more.

My first 50 miler was finished. It was hilly and epic fun. There were highs, in fields of inquisitive horses, and lows as I died a little at each additional stile or stuck cattle gate. I'd learnt a lot and knew where I needed to improve.

Advice on Increasing Mileage

When you first start running, your focus is likely to be on the time you spend on feet as you make the journey to becoming a regular runner. Once you've made the change from sofa dweller to runner, the focus switches to distance as you prepare for events and gradually increase the miles.

In my own running I've slowly increased weekly mileage over the years, sticking to the 10 per cent increase per week maximum and have been largely injury-free. Some of this is luck, as on any run, or even walking to work you could twist an ankle, but overall the slow increasing has been successful.

The best way to improve your times is with consistent, uninterrupted quality training. You can't improve while injured so don't push too hard. Legs will hurt but actual pain is a sign something is wrong.

YEAR 1

I first started running, gradually increased and managed first 5k, 10k, three half marathons and (just) my first marathon with a of 4h57m. Across the year I averaged 13 miles per week, a figure that would have been unimaginable at the start of the journey.

YEAR 2

I joined a MK Lakeside Runners to prepare for London and Milton Keynes Marathons, a week apart. Then I got carried away and ran 12 marathons average time of 4h06m, best of 3h49m off of 30 miles per week – a big jump in mileage but made under watchful eye of the club coaches.

YEAR 3

Tackled a Quadzilla event (four marathons in four days) and started pushing for a higher number of marathons. Ran 19 marathons, average time of 4h02m, best of 3h37m. I ran more events but trained less and towards the end of the year my times got steadily worse. Averaged 30 miles per week.

YEAR 4

I decided to aim for quality over quantity and ran only 18 marathons. Increasing mileage to an average of 33 per week seemed to make a difference, and my average of 18 marathons dropped to 3h41m with a best of 3h27, finally breaking sub 3h30m.

YEAR 5

I undertook my second Quadzilla on the way to 18 marathons again. Average dropped to 3h38, with a 3h24m best. The back half of my year went amazingly well and I managed to PB on three marathons in the space of six weeks, largely down to increasing mileage to 38 per week. The main difference to training was adding a hard nine-mile tempo session (run at a fast pace for sustained effort) on a Wednesday morning with the Redway Runners. Pushing yourself on legs tired from interval work the previous night builds endurance and stubbornness.

YEAR 6

I decided to make a conscious effort to ramp up the mileage as I started looking towards ultra events (longer than marathon distance), managing to hit 200 mile months throughout the year to complete over 2,500 miles in total. My weekly mileage jumped to 48 on average with a marathon PB of 3h15m. My average for the year was only marginally improved to 3h36m but I often ran on tired legs from my first 38 and 50 milers. Despite the mileage I managed to PB at every distance from 5k upwards which was reassuring I wasn't sacrificing endurance for speed.

YEAR 7

I didn't want to maintain the 200 mile months specifically, but with my first 100-mile race planned knew I needed to keep my mileage up. Ran a 40 and a 50 miler in preparation, along with a third Quadzilla to get the back-to-back runs in. I kept my weekly mileage around the 48–50 point until May when I pushed it to 75–85 a week in final preparation, hitting 300 miles for the month. In June I took on the South Downs Way 100 as my 97th marathon and then switched focus back to marathons for the final few races before my 100th in September. After that, a last-minute entry saw me try for a second 100-mile event at the Autumn 100. My final mileage for the year was over 2,600 as a result. I know people that drive less far in a year.

24

ACCIDENTAL ULTRA

January 2017 – Ranscombe Challenge

Sometimes your goal can change mid-event, often because you've gone off too fast and your planned PB is replaced with 'just finish without dying'. Other times a change can be more pragmatic.

One early Saturday morning in Kent I registered in a field at the gorgeous Ranscombe country park, ready to knock marathon 88 off the list. The event was organised by Saxons, Vikings & Normans Marathons who arrange a lot of small friendly events, mostly in the Kent area. They can be a bit of a drive from MK but this one was just over the Dartford bridge and in a great setting: an eight-hour challenge with every runner completing as many 4.5-mile laps as they want in the allotted time. Three laps made a half marathon, six for a marathon.

This style of event is great for anyone nervous about

a single loop marathon or coming back from injury. Provided you finish one lap you get a medal so there's no pressure of a Did Not Finish. Most runners find they're capable of far more than they expect. If having doubt, they can take a break at the aid station, consider another lap and continue or not, all in a no pressure format.

I hadn't run the course before and it was beautiful, frozen solid for the first couple of hours which helped keep the mud down. Despite a relatively light week of training I found all the hills a struggle from early on – once again, MK is too flat – and quickly realised that I wouldn't achieve a decent marathon time. Given the choice of a disappointing marathon or an unplanned ultra I decided to make the most of the great weather and run some extra laps. The main advantage was that, on an ultra, no one is expected to walk the hills. This gave me an excuse not to kill myself up the inclines. 'No, I'm not rubbish at hills but thanks for asking. I'm actually doing the ultra.' Due to the varied nature of the course my splits were all over the place and on single laps I recorded both pace from blistering fast to slower than granny walks.

As the course warmed up the mud thawed and under-foot conditions varied from clinging clay that added inches to your height, to sloppy grip-free mush that defeated all attempts to gain traction. Hitting a HM in two hours and a full marathon in just over four I started to fade for the first of the 'optional' laps. I adopted the 'walk and eat' approach to replicate the longer ultra strategy, and perked up after some Coke (the liquid kind not the illicit sort), knocking out two more to hit 39 miles in 6h55m. The one stipulation on the event is you must start your final lap inside seven hours, so I could conceivably go out again. I was first to finish nine laps and was briefly the distance winner until the guy behind me went out for a tenth. I was sorely tempted to go after him, but common sense prevailed. I retired at second place on distance at 39 miles and averaged 10:38minute/ mile pace, a good training run for the SDW50 and SDW100 later in year.

Making the long runs count – Warm-up distances

As your race distances increase you may find that your regular events aren't sufficient for training. As much as you love your local parkrun, a 5k run when training for a half marathon or longer isn't going to cut it. If you can't bear the thought of missing your friends and the post-run cake at the café, a good tip is to get a run in before you hit the parkrun for some speedwork. Since you won't be going for a PB it doesn't matter if you're a minute or two late. Simply catch the tail runner and (politely) work through the field, focusing on picking off the runners ahead. It should recreate the later stages of a marathon where your expert training, pacing and endurance means you're still gaining places and powering towards the end while many around you are blowing up and struggling for the last few miles.

If you are adding distance to a formal race where you need to register and collect timing chips, etc., then allow time for this. It will mean a more broken run as you stop for 10–20 minutes to get ready and pin numbers on but is still a great way of getting miles in. It's not uncommon to see those running half marathons do some warm-up miles to get closer to the marathon distance they're training for. In an overly ambitious move I decided a 16 mile warm-up to the inaugural (and excellent) Buckingham HM would be ideal ultra training. It worked but was a close-run thing, with me nearly missing the race being lost somewhere between MK and Buckingham. It was worth it all for the post-race cake though.

25

I WOULD WALK 100 MILES
(I'M NOT AS FAST AS
THE PROCLAIMERS)

My 7th year of running included my 100th marathon and my first attempt at 100 miles. Marathons had felt daunting at the start, when I struggled to complete 5k. I kept reminding myself of this when training for 100 miles.

The main downside of a 100 mile event is that there is no handy euphemism. You can use the word 'marathon' and forget what a marathon is: 26.2 long miles of running, and painful legs. It's just a 'marathon' after all, keep calm. But 100 miles is always 100 miles. 100 of anything is a big number. Eating 100 Maltesers would be a significant undertaking. Running 100 miles is plain stupid.

Just how stupid was emphasised as friends and colleagues learned of my plans. They'd look at me in an odd manner, ask for clarification and wonder if I'd confused the units of measurement 'You mean 100 metres?'

Those that could get their head around the distance presumed it was a multi-day event with periods of rest in between. Sadly not. This would be 100 miles, non-stop in one go.

Knowing that I wanted to run my first 100 with Centurion Running because of the amazing support they provide runners, and after being bullied into it by Jen, I chose the South Downs Way 100. Of the four available 100 mile events I was initially tempted by the Thames Path 100 (sounds flat, right?) but realised it was the same weekend as the Milton Keynes Marathon and I didn't want to end my attendance streak. Even walking 26.2 miles straight after a 100 miler would be out of the question, so I settled on the SDW100 instead. 100 miles from Winchester to Eastbourne, as the name suggests, the route largely follows the South Downs Way national trail so navigation was less of an issue.

As preparation I entered the South Downs Way 50, which covers the final 50 miles of the 100, starting at Worthing and ending at Eastbourne. This seemed an ideal way to practise the second half of the course and tackle any of the difficult navigation sections while still (relatively) fresh.

Halfway Practice – Preparing for the South Downs Way 50

As for the CW50, I made the same geeky table of check-points and paces to ensure I'd be on pace and avoid any disasters. Cut-off was the same 13 hours and I hoped for a time of around nine to ten hours. The elevation gain of 5,700ft or 1,750m was only marginally more than the 5,600ft or 1,700m at the CW50 as well. Considering the timings from the CW50 gave me some idea of average overall pace, so I could make an estimate of expected arrival times at each point. With a 9am start I hoped to be done by 6.30pm and hopefully not need the head torch, although I carried two as mandatory kit required (one as a backup).

Unlike the CW50, which showed more or less even average splits across the course, SDW50 included a much slower section to Housedean Farm, then a quicker next section, indicating a steep ascent followed by a descent. While ignorance is often bliss, if you're struggling up a monster hill at mile 20 of 50, it can be reassuring to know that it's the worst bit of the course and not typical of the remaining 30 miles.

Many races of any distance are out and back routes, or a number of loops, to simplify the logistics of bag drop and getting to and from the event. SDW50 is basically a straight line, so the *fun* of the event is to finish 50 miles from your parked car. You could view this as an excuse for bonus miles and run back, but for the sound of mind this is not an option. Centurion Running provide a bus service for a good price but it doesn't leave until after the race cut-off. Given that Jen and I were hoping to run around nine hours, and cut-off was 13 hours, we would have to endure up to four hours of waiting when all we wanted was to get home to bed. We elected to take the train back to the start, but Southern Rail went on strike and we were reduced to taxis. It's worth planning the logistics of races ahead, to allow for eventualities like this, and to ensure your drop bag is suitable for lugging up and down train station stairs with knackered legs.

Pace plans were also influenced by my goal for the 100 mile event. Many previous runners had recommended aiming to break 100 miles into four sections of 25 and aiming for sections to take four, five, six and seven hours (22 hours total) or five, six, seven and eight hours (26 hours total) to account for fade. Planning to come in under 24 hours for the 100, I aimed for nine hours for the 50. This left scope for further fade in the uncharted territory of the big one.

Despite awful weather in the preceding months, the few weeks prior to the SDW50 were great. Reports from locals confirmed that the course had dried to a rock-hard rutted state. Many trail shoes have little cushioning so were deemed by locals insufficient to protect feet from being 'ripped to bits' on the chalky flint surface. Phrases like this do little to steady the nerves. I leant towards cushioned road shoes with a fair bit of grip, in case any muddy sections popped up.

The next area of doubt was what to wear. Running can be more fraught with clothing decisions than a first date. The early onset of spring brought rising temperatures and the weekend was forecast to be the hottest of the year, maybe topping 23°C. Given that most UK runners had been training in single digits, this increase was akin to being relocated to the desert. Running a final 20 miles the week before, while carrying full kit to check for issues and wearing compression top and tee, I had felt good. Now I wondered if I'd need a change of plan. A quick check of the event Facebook group confirmed that many who had run before warned it would be colder 'up along the ridge' or 'down in the deep valley'.

Ridge? Valley? This sounded more like the ascent of a mountain range than the scenic dawdle through fields that I'd envisaged.

The combination of footwear, temperature and scary mountain phrases induced some last-minute wobbles of confidence, which weren't helped by a more extensive mandatory kit list than the last 50 mile event. Requirements this time included not only two head torches (implying you might be stuck out there for so long one would be insufficient) but also a hat, gloves and spare long-sleeved top. Gulp.

Comedy relief unwittingly arrived with the excellent decision Centurion Running made to go cupless at aid stations. I'm not sure how many cups they go through, but it would be considerable with 400 runners and six stations. From 2017 they elected to add cups to the kit list. You carry your own.

Several running equipment suppliers stock folding/collapsing cups, so a ceramic Horlicks mug is not required. I ordered one from Salomon without registering the size. It was £6 for a cup and, since it was called a cup, I figured it must be about the size of a cup, with similar volume to say, a cup. What arrived had a capacity equal to a contact lens case. It was of sufficient size to catch the tears of a small, morose sparrow. I envisaged a dozen or so refills at each aid station, requesting that the volunteers 'hit me again' like a bar drunk drowning his sorrows but with mouthfuls of cola and sports drink in place of bourbon. More experienced runners mentioned that a Capri Sun pouch with the top cut off is bigger and cheaper.

Running the South Downs Way 50

Race day approached, and I'd repacked my bag more times than I'd like to admit. The weather report was 'hot' so I tried my best to trim unwanted weight. Sadly, when you're a chunky size there's a limit to how small a waterproof jacket and long-sleeved base layer will go. After picking Jen up at an ungodly hour we travelled to Worthing, stopping for breakfast in the services. I was keen to improve on my tried-and-tested formula and added a bacon roll to my sausage and egg bagel from McDonald's. Jen had coffee and the most unappealing granola mush I've ever seen before we got back on the road, alternately passing through dense fog and bright morning sunshine, unsure which would be more conducive to a decent race.

Race HQ was at Worthing college, which the SatNav got us most of the way to before abandoning us in a tiny lane. After picking up a passing runner who looked like he knew where he was going (he didn't) we arrived and registered, all set to go. Time for a last-minute shoe choice (stick with road shoes, trust the random internet advice), and the application of sunscreen. I threw on my 'maybe I'll pack this just in case' running cap ready to shuffle off to the inflatable starting arch and the safety briefing.

At the end of the briefing they did a special mention for the 'grand slammers', those attempting all four of the Centurion 50-mile challenges in a single year and the double slammers, those attempting all four of the 100-mile events as well. We set off across the sports field and up the lane on route to the South Downs trail itself.

The first section is congested which helps to hold pace back. After a few miles I was keeping pace with Jen and trotting along through hills that seemed quite gentle. We were both glad we stuck with road shoes, finding that chalky soil baked rock-hard by the sun is less 'giving' than tarmac. I had a broad plan of four hours and five hours for each half to match my intended 100 mile pace.

Miles one to three passed in a blur but I noticed sweat beading and dropping from my cap. It was hot, so I kept drinking to stay ahead of the fluid loss. On some sections we almost ran too fast due to the easy nature of the trail, but held back to enjoy the views. To the right were clear skies as far as we could see and to the left, the thick fog we saw on the drive down, still clinging to low-lying ground.

Later, a marshal let Jen know that she was 6th lady. Jen is by nature competitive and the first signs of the inner battle to hold back or battle it out for pace started to show. She tried to at least look like she was ignoring it: a losing battle like Bruce Banner trying to keep the Hulk at bay. Coming into the first aid station at Botolphs we had covered 11 miles and were gaining on the 5th lady. Climbing the steep hill after the aid station I was choking on an ill-chosen sausage roll as she went full-Hulk and shot up over the hill into the distance with a finish position in mind. I just hoped I wouldn't die by party-sized pork product. What a rubbish way to DNF the race that would be.

Passing the YHA at Truleigh Hill I was greeted by a tempting sign advertising ice cream but made do with tepid sports drinks and kept on. The path had been wide and open for many miles but started to narrow through trees. The dot of Jen in the distance was gone for good. The Saddlescombe aid station came soon after, at 17 miles: over a third of the total distance. Helpful marshals filled my water bottles while I wrestled with the stupid collapsing cup. Fearful of another near-death, savoury food incident I confined my food consumption to the fruit.

After some more fields, we crossed the A23 where a petrol station hovered fleetingly within reach. Ever noticed how BP always have the aircon turned nice and low? That would feel so good about now. Putting it to the back of my mind I noticed a group of hikers up ahead, widely enough spread to block the entire road through the village, swinging their walking poles without a care in the world. I got some speed up and politely weaved through before the path narrowed to a bare shoulder-width between thick bushes. Once again, my experience came into play so I wouldn't get stuck behind... Horses? Where the hell had they come from?

With over a hundred miles of the South Downs Way to gallop, here were two horses on the narrowest section. They were such massive lumps that their horsey bums barely scraped between the bushes.

I don't have strong feelings about horses either way, it's just unfortunate that one of the biggest creatures in the UK has the mental capacity of a slow-witted mouse and is prone to bolting if something like a carrier bag stuck in a tree makes a sudden movement.

Other runners caught up, all unsure about the acceptable approach. The road was so close I debated leaping through thick bushes to chance the traffic, which meant the riders and horses couldn't hear us. Should we shout and risk two horseshoe imprints to the chest?

Fortunately, the riders pulled over to let some oncoming cyclists pass. Seeing our sweaty visages, the cyclists elected to pull to the side and a slow procession of stinking runners muttered a quiet 'thank you' as we squeezed past.

At the next road crossing, the group elected a 'volunteer' to step into the traffic and take one for the team so the rest could cross. We eventually climbed past Pyecombe Golf Club, joined by some more cyclists and, after a further climb, approached Ditchling Beacon Nature Reserve where the car park was packed with people enjoying the sun and supporting the runners. We were greeted by claps and cheers as we passed. I entirely missed the ice cream van that was probably serving the best cone with flake for miles around, and had a squashed energy bar instead.

Centurion had done well to signpost the next few

miles where the South Downs Way makes a series of seemingly random turns as it zigzags across the hills. My pace was still on track and, coming up to halfway just over four hours I was only slightly behind the planned four/five split. The sun was relentless, and I'd drained my bottles. At ten miles this is the longest gap between aid stations and I was feeling it.

One bit of ultra advice that sticks out is to remember everything is temporary. If you feel good, go for it as you'll feel rubbish later. If you feel like death, ignore it as it will pass.

Coming into woods section I was caught by a runner who warned me that the next section was a 'F*cking stupid bit. Really stupid. Don't know what they were thinking.' I am not sure if he meant the event organisers or the original users of the South Downs Way, but the steep climb in the woods was certainly enough to slow progress to a painful walk. Before bursting out of the trees on a long downhill prior to hitting the Housedean aid station at 26.6 miles, I had drained every drop of fluid.

Watching me chugging back tiny thimbles of Pepsi, the volunteers topped up my bottles again with sports drink. Feeling this thirsty, I was happy to accept whatever flavour they offered but immediately regretted it when I discovered that, whatever it was, it tasted like sweaty arse. It could well be that sweat had got into the mouthpieces, but the fruity refreshing goodness of the other flavours had been replaced with 'builder's bum on a summer day'.

Climbing from the aid station and crossing the A27

there was a large sign advertising a wedding party down the road. I was sure a Pimms would go down great. Would it be frowned upon to gate-crash in running gear?

Starting the long climb to Castle Hill, I attempted various methods of increasing forward momentum. I couldn't manage a run on the slopes, but walking was too slow. A sort of compromise shuffle, reminiscent of an old man rushing for a bus but not sure enough of his footing to break into a jog, worked, and I passed a few runners as we approached a herd of cows in a field. A field we had to enter. I love cows when there's a sturdy fence between us, and it's entirely coincidental that I slowed to allow other runners to catch me.

Cows are officially the deadliest animal in the UK and kill twice as many people as dogs. They're more deadly than sharks and, given that we were several hundred metres above sea level, more relevant. If one of the blood-crazed homicidal cows chose to attack I now had a reduced chance of being the victim. Tactfully keeping a sacrificial runner between myself and the bovine murderers we jogged through the field, passing as close to the cows as we dared to limit excess mileage but avoiding the more recalcitrant individuals who looked spoiling for a fight. Most just stared at us, some ran away (phew!), some stumbled towards us with murder in their eyes. Or they may have just been nosy and wanted a pat. Fortunately we made it through and with a cattle gate safely between us could resume running with only rabbits and crows for company.

After more weaving, the footpath joined a hard concrete road that passes between oil seed rape fields.

The road was level or downhill, and presented a great opportunity to pick off some distance at a decent pace, making the most of the cushioning on my road shoes. It continued to South Farm before a sharp turn alongside an impressive pile of manure, all the better to clear the airways before a short climb to Southease rail station and the leg-burning footbridge crossing the train line. After 33 miles of hills, two simple staircases were torture, especially the descent.

Southease aid station meant there was only 16 miles to go. Fuelled by more, better tasting energy drink and with a handful of fruit, I did the sums. Keeping below 12-minute miles I'd be just over nine but still under my previous 50 mile time: doable.

The climb carried on. And on. One false summit after another arrived but 'I'll run once we reach the top' never did. My willingness to run was dampened by a belly full of Pepsi that felt wobbly and bursting with gas that took a good few minutes of discomfort to release. Still climbing, I fell in with another runner who had done the race before. He agreed we were on just over nine-hour pace, and he regaled me with stories of hitting the same hill 74 miles into the SDW100 race, in the fog, at night, blindly following markers and the lights of other runners, and being startled by sudden appearance of cows. He had completed the 100 in under 23 hours, which was some reassurance that I might manage the same in June.

Eventually, the hill ran out of false summits and we achieved a decent pace along the gentle slope remaining. Up ahead was a massive TV mast at Firle Beacon, towering over the countryside. Logically, this must be the top of the highest hill so we were due a bit of downhill on the other side. The going was good with soft grass either side of the path, and I clocked some decent miles at around 8minute/mile pace. The nine-hour target was now somewhere between 11:30 and 12:00minute/mile pace. I could maybe still do this.

At 41 miles the path changed from gently downhill to potholed steep drive, and my knackered quads started to complain. Nine miles left. That's the same as a Wednesday run if you ignore the 41-mile warm-up.

Leaving the aid station I remembered that the first of the trickier navigation sections was coming up. I'd watched the video on the event website and had notes in my bag, but didn't need them as the route was clearly marked. In a brainwave I realised I was still carrying weight I didn't need. Ditching extra food into the bushes for the wildlife to enjoy, I stashed the wrappers for later disposal. I must have dropped only about 100g but it felt good.

The path climbed towards Windover Hill and the Long Man of Wilmington, a sixteenth-century chalk figure cut into the side of the hill. He's 72 metres tall and holds two walking poles, or 'cheat sticks' as they're known in trail running. Right now, I could do with a borrow of said sticks, or his 35-metre legs to assist my old man shuffle up the path. There simply weren't enough miles to make up for slowing down but I was walking the last section when a passing runner asked if I was injured as my right leg looked odd. No, mate, that's just how I walk. Six years of running have cured one duck leg but my right still points to the side like it's contemplating a different course.

When the hill eventually ended I 'jogged' off to make up time. My feet were barely skimming the path, refusing to rise higher, and I reminded myself that if the original fat fella (I use a stronger word that also starts with 'f' and rhymes with 'duck') version of me can wobble his bum between lamp posts, ignoring the aches and pains, then older, wiser, lighter me is not going to let him down now.

With around four miles to go, distance was becoming critical.

Redeeming itself, my brain came up with a master plan: lighten weight further. I was carrying over 1kg of water but the weather was cooling, and only a little further than a parkrun meant the end and bountiful rehydration. I emptied both bottles over the next half mile, but not by tipping them out as would have been sensible. No, I chose to drink them, successfully lightening my race vest by 1kg but adding 1kg to my swollen belly: a net weight change of zero. Genius.

Thundering down the final gulley towards civilisation my pace built again but was erratic due to tree roots, narrow sections and thick, evil bushes. It would be easy to come a cropper on tired legs. Two miles left and 28 minutes. If I could avoid mistakes, I had this!

The path broke onto a suburban street and I was feeling good. An easily missed right-turn into an alley was just where I expected it to be, no one was coming up behind. The runners had spread over the last few miles and I was on my own. Breaking out of the alley onto Willingdon Road I almost crashed into the barrier designed to stop idiots like me running onto the road. This was another tricky section, but I was pretty sure. An arrow on the floor pointed left. Pace steady, there was little that could stop me getting under nine hours. I was tired but forced myself to watch for the next marker. No way was I getting lost now.

A passing car honked. A lot. An awful lot. The driver leant out the window and wildly gesticulated that I'd missed the turning. My brain slowly registered the noise as words and I turned to see two runners pop out of the alley, cross the road and make a turn I had missed. They seemed in no doubt of the route and were making for home. Two places lost and added extra distance!

Obviously, I have the navigational ability of a wasp stuck in a window.

Swearing at myself that the sensible option was to gain on the runners and stay with them, after a burst of speed I grimly held on as long as possible. Rounding the hospital, I saw the athletics track ahead and knew there was literally a 400-metre lap to go. I felt like taking it easy but with a final spurt (upon realising that a sub 8h50m was possible) I crossed the line.

It had been gruelling, but by running when able, grinding away on the steep sections, and shuffling up the easier climbs, I'd managed to knock 45 minutes off my previous 50 mile time.

After finding Jen, who finished 4th lady, a few seconds outside eight hours despite a marathon PB the week before, I shuffled to the showers to contemplate how to remove trainers and calf guards when I couldn't bend to reach past my knees.

I'd managed to come in under my nine-hour target. Come the 100 mile version, if I stayed on plan, I'd have six hours for the next 25 miles and seven hours for the final section. At home on the sofa with fresh legs, seven hours seemed like no great effort, but I was unsure how easy it would feel with 75 miles already covered.

Final Planning – South Downs Way 100

The step up to 100 miles from 50 is considerable. Doubling the distance is no small feat, and the cut-off for SDW100 going from 13 hours for the 50 mile event to 30 hours is a measure of how much the extra distance can take a toll on pace. Even the winners were expected to take a whole 14 hours to finish, against six hours for the half distance. The elevation gain is 12,700ft or 4,000m, more than twice that of the SDW50 so indicating a fair bit more climb in the first half.

The longer distance also allows runners to have a drop bag available at the halfway point, and at 76 miles, so you can change kit or have a particular vital foodstuff available. Maybe a new pair of legs?

My main goal was to finish, running at an average pace of 18minute/mile. That sounds ridiculously easy on paper, approaching the pace of a gentle wander through the supermarket. In reality, I expected this to be extremely hard as tiredness and the need to eat real food would likely kick in.

Finishers get a massive belt buckle to impress their neighbours and friends. I'm not sure where it started but belt buckles are big in American ultras and common for events over 100 miles. For the SDW the buckle features the Centurion logo, the race name and '100 mile Finisher' below it. They have an extra incentive for finishers under 24 hours who receive a special '100 miles – One Day' version of the buckle. That was the one I wanted. It looks the same and unless someone is reading your crotch makes no real difference, but it was better and harder, so I wanted it.

26

RUNNING 100 MILES, OR ATTEMPTING TO

Final thoughts

After months of training (and trying to ignore the impending race) SDW100 was fast approaching. I was, by now, confident of shoes and other kit. Pace-wise, after a lot of guesswork, I knocked up a rough timings chart with crucial cut-off times and toilet locations, and added the crew locations as additional waypoints.

Given that I had now achieved under 3h30m on most marathons, and was disappointed with any mile time that started with an 8, planning a race where 10min/mile was the fastest and likely to drop to 18:30min/miles was a sobering thought.

Final prep for a 100 miler is a lot more involving than for a marathon. Along with the usual drop bag for the end, you have the option of two smaller drop bags (or shoeboxes) at 50 and 75 miles. Contents can range from your perfect race food to a change of kit. The more you pack the more time you're likely to lose at aid stations messing with stuff unnecessarily, and the longer you spend stationary the harder it will be to get going again. By Tuesday I'd got as far as labelling two empty shoeboxes with my race number while trying to imagine what I'd want to eat at 75 miles that would see me to the finish.

They say ultras are run with the head not the body (good job I have a MASSIVE head then). So, in an effort to focus on positive aspects, I made a list of why I was going to finish:

1. Ran four marathons back to back over four days in training.

2. Ran SDW50 (the latter half of the SDW100) in April so I knew the route and terrain.

3. Had run 200+ miles a month for prior 17 months, culminating in 300+ for May.

4. Had tested all my kit at the SDW50 and several training runs.

5. Broke my new shoes in running in Spanish hills.

6. My lovely wife was crewing me and, after 20 years, knew me better than I knew myself.

7. Paced clubmate Chris through the night section of the GUCR145 race two weeks prior so had experience of running from dusk to dawn.

8. I'm as stubborn as my dad. I've never DNF'd

before.

9. Actually tapered semi-properly.

10. I'd given up caffeine for two weeks. Coke could now likely propel me better than the powdered illegal version.

11. I'm a fatty. I have enough energy reserves to keep me going for months.

Friday

After dropping our children with the in-laws, we headed to Winchester. With no pacers, Cloë was fulfilling the unenviable task of crewing me for 100 miles though moods were likely to range from jubilation to 'I hate the sky, I hate that tree, even the footpath is a miserable devil, kill me now.'

The usual Friday traffic was not too bad. With kit check and registration complete, I handed over my two shoe boxes as drop bags. Head torches don't have to be carried until 54 miles, so they went in along with a spare top and a cheap charity vest that I could bin at the next stop. I expected to get to the 76.6 stop at Housedean around 10pm, and figured that this would be when the temperature dropped. I packed a long-sleeved hooded top and a further base layer and, in both boxes, stuck in an iced coffee for a caffeine boost.

Planning a schedule had been tricky with pace ranging from 10min/mile to 18:30 hobble. Unlike marathons where I always set off too fast and optimistically hope not to fade, I knew this run would go from 'hold back' to 'hold on', and night sections were a guess, probably ending up at 'hold me'.

It was now just a matter of dinner (massive burger and beer) with Steve, Jen and Andy and a final food stop at Tesco for breakfast essentials.

Saturday

Up at 4.30 to dress. Ultra-running is great. You get up at a stupid hour to force down food (egg and bacon buttie from Tesco as too early for hotel breakfast), slather yourself liberally with sun cream and Vaseline before pulling on unattractive Lycra leisurewear you just pray isn't going to rub you raw. Mild panic set in when, in reception, I realised I'd left my race bib back in the room and would have to wake my sleeping wife to retrieve it before catching the taxi to the starting field.

So, to begin.

With less than a mile covered I was sweating like a drug mule at the border. It wasn't hot yet, but something was not right. Trying to stay calm I put it down to nerves, not dwelling on the fact I was tired from a 1.5 mile fun run with my daughter the day before. This could mean I had a bug or something. Wisely I backed off, let Jen go, and ran with Steve for a while. Consciously walking all the inclines and holding back on the flat I started to feel better.

Somewhere between loo stops I lost touch with Steve

so I was on my own for the next 95 miles, although in a group of runners all going the same steady pace. A moment of panic followed in Exton when a competitor ran back towards our group swearing we'd gone off course. Despite visible route markings ahead and several runners having completed the event before, he would not be convinced and ran into the distance never to be seen again.

Our first aid stop arrived at 9.8 miles at Beacon Hill. Having read a few blogs advising that there is a big gap between two of the early stations I'd packed a backup empty bottle, but was sure that this wasn't the relevant gap. Grabbing a handful of fruit from the table I blasted through. Sadly, I was wrong about the stations. This *was* the big gap. Nearly a half marathon between stops meant I was down to the last few drops by Queen Elizabeth County Park after 3h47m (a mere minute behind my schedule), where I hit the Coke supply hard.

Volunteers packing up the local parkrun cheered me on as I wandered past with a sandwich bag full of fruit. I'd resolved to never eat at the stations, just fill a bag and go. Normally I'd have left the fruit as a last resort, but this time it's all I fancy. I am pretty sure that if I'd bottled my pee, I could have sold it as a fruit smoothie.

Still making a conscious effort to walk all the hills, I felt strong. Coming up to marathon distance at that point I didn't feel that I had been on any real hills despite the course profile. Only one long run down Butser hill really gave the impression of how far we'd climbed. Twenty miles in 3h45m, 25 miles in 4h23m. I passed 33.3 miles at 6h01m and started some cheesy windswept videos on Facebook to force me to keep my pace steady. Comments and encouragement were great and helped keep me walking where needed.

At 35 miles the course hits Cocking. I was met by a smiling Cloë who helped me refuel and only gagged slightly upon receiving my sweaty base layer and tee. I carried on with just a fresh tee.

Jen was apparently running great, having taken a tumble that had done nothing to slow her. With 6h21m gone I was behind schedule by around 20 minutes; I'd planned 23hrs to give some comfort of going sub 24. I'd used a third of the safety margin within a third of the race, and I fade HORRIBLY in every race of every distance.

My mind was taken off the issue of timing when I next stopped for a wee. Despite proven shorts and lots of Vaseline, adjustment of the man equipment demonstrated that something was not right. I had some undercarriage rubbing which was not nice. With a crew stop at Amberley coming up I messaged Cloë to bring lots and lots of Vaseline. Even adopting a slightly waddle stride to save the knackers kept my pace too high so unfortunately I beat the car to the crew station and waddled onto the next one. 47.4 miles down.

The next checkpoint was at 50.1 where crew are not allowed. A bag full of fruit and more energy drink and I pushed on. Sadly, I got the 'natural' flavour which still haunted me from the SDW50, so topped up with Coke to take the edge off. Aid stations are seldom further than eight or nine miles apart and I was getting through over a litre of fluids between, to fight the sun. Drinking lots to avoid dehydration, my painful wee stops were increasingly frequent. If I was to DNF due to boys' bits issues, I would struggle to see the funny side.

On the plus side, this was now the furthest I've ever run. Fifty had been my max so every step was a new distance personal best. It also meant I needed to run another 50 miles. Another 50 bloody miles... I'd been running for 9h25m so...still a decent buffer for sub 24hrs. Running the first half 35 minutes slower than the SDW50 meant I was physically in a better place if I ignored the fact that I might be rubbing my appendage away and end up a Ken doll.

Chantry Post at 51.2miles was my salvation, along with Cloë and the big tub of Vaseline. Issue sorted, I ran on to the major aid station and my drop bag.

It's odd to run into a village hall, hundreds of miles from home, to be greeted by two MK locals doing the timekeeping, and great to see the friendly faces of Sheila and Russell Rose cheering runners in. Sheila is a clean-eating personal trainer, extolling the virtues of mini-malist footwear, strength and conditioning work and a healthy vegan diet. She's pretty much the opposite of me who's yet to meet a vegetable as appealing as a steak.

After a wet wipe down, I donned a dry base layer and my Bad Boy Running Podcast top. Hoping that some volunteer support would keep me going, I learned of a local runner and fellow listener, also called Russell, who was willing to give up some of his Saturday to run with a stranger.

I could be an axe murderer. He could be an axe murderer. Maybe being chased by an axe-wielding murderer would get me going.

Head torches packed away, I binned the drop box, received a kiss from Cloë and set off again. The climb out of Washington was a drag and the stop had stolen some oomph from my legs that the espresso tried to return. Only 22 minutes behind schedule arriving at the aid station I was further behind leaving it, even with what felt like a quick change.

My salvation arrived in the form of a loud 'F*ck You Buddy' (the traditional Bad Boy Running Podcast greeting for some reason) when Russell popped up ahead. We shared a manly hug during which he managed to avoid reeling back from my sweaty stink. Company really helps and, although I was less than chatty, we cruised along at a decent pace, at times managing sections at speeds that have eluded me in later stages of badly judged marathons.

At Botolphs he had to bid me farewell and leave to enjoy the rest of the weekend with someone who does not smell like a hobo, but he helped me make up a lot of time in that section, and accompanied me well onto the route I knew from the SDW50. I was on familiar ground from this point. He did make me regret not sorting more pacers, but it was always a toss-up between manning it out on my own and having someone hold my hand.

Sixty-one miles passes in 12hrs dead, only ten minutes behind schedule.

At the top of the climb from Botolphs at Truleigh Hills I reached the youth hostel I'd clocked on the SDW50. This time I had cash in hand when it came into view. I bumped into another runner inside and we debated which ice cream would get us through the evening. You don't get opportunities like this on a marathon. He went for Magnum, but it's easier to hike without having to bite around a stick, praying you finish it before it melts and falls off. Your race would likely end right there, kneeling on the floor, digging in the dirt for the vanilla goodness, beseeching your god(s) against this cruellest of punishments. In short, I'm more of a Calippo man.

Hitting the Devil's Dyke climb, the route came back to me when I recalled running this section with Jen. I picked up the pace and hit the pub at the top of the hill at 13h15m, then realised there isn't a pub on the 50. I was lost.

Bugger. My good wife was on the course, unlike me, and after a quick call I got back on route, having lost about five minutes.

Saddlescombe Farm came up at the devilish 66.6 miles (or more like 67 if you're a f*ck nugget who gets lost and just runs to the nearest pub). Food still did not appeal but a small shot of rice pudding seemed to sit well. I figured nothing but fruit for 100 miles was likely to lead to a bum explosion of epic proportions. I had never had a toilet issue before, but had never run 67 miles either.

Ditchling Beacon arrived at 72 miles. There was an ice cream van here on the 50 but not this time as it was after 8pm. Instead, there was another welcome appearance of Cloë, this time with a McDonald's and a slushy drink. For the first time in my life I declined the McDonald's (had I declined a bit more often in the last 30 years I might not have needed to run 100 miles), grabbed the drink and a kiss and set off to Housedean Farm and the second drop box only around seven minutes behind schedule.

The wood section just before Housedean arrived as the light began to fade. My head torch was still in the bag, but I wanted to push on and, somehow, got through without tripping on any roots. Instead, I tripped on the descent down into Housedean Farm, teetering on the point of face planting for what felt like a lifetime.

They say an ultra is run in your head and that doubts hit with nightfall, and they are right. I just needed to finish this stupid thing and go home. With nearly eight hours left to break 24 hours, and 14 before the cut-off I could pretty much walk in. Thirty-minute miles would see me finish before the cut-off, but it all seemed point-less and I would rather have been in the pub with a beer.

A few mental games (I don't HAVE to run across the hills at night, I GET to run across the countryside on a clear, warm evening, enjoying nature and seeing what cows look like asleep) saw me through. Luckily a few runners caught up and we met another lost on the top of the hill. With a combination of my route experience and a GPS file on someone's watch, we determined the route and pushed on. There seemed oddly little marking for a Centurion event and a few miles later we possibly found the reason: two kids on dirt bikes were hammering around the hills, no lights, no crash helmets and prob-ably no licence either, with mischief in their eyes.

Sunday (Still running...)

We ran as a group, but differing paces meant we eventually split. I ended up running ahead with a lady called Kathleen along the 'yellow brick road', the concrete road between the oil seed rape fields. It's hard on the knees but good not to have to judge every step and look for flints and ankle snapping potholes. Sadly, the pace meant we flew past the turning for the South Downs Way, downhill into a field of cows where, by chance, we woke a dozing calf who ran in alarm ahead of us. The mother followed us behind, concerned about what we were doing with her offspring. We were trapped between calf and mum, wondering how much a cow kick hurts but, taking our head torches off, managed to sneak past and continue to Iford, three villages away from Southease, which was where we should have been.

In a second master stroke we ran towards Swanborough, the wrong way again, before realising the mistake and finally heading back to Southease and the railway crossing, reaching the aid station having enjoyed over two bonus miles of calf chasing, car dodging fun. When you've been on your feet 18 hours and covered 86 miles it's a mental challenge not to hail a passing cab and go home. 100 miles is a long way to run; 102 seems a lot further.

Focusing on the positives, and after an unexpected and morale-boosting extra visit by Cloë, I found I was only 12 minutes behind schedule. Just after midnight we had 16 miles to cover in six hours for the 24hr buckle, or ten hours for the cut-off. Somewhere before Alfriston

Kathleen fell back with some other runners, while I power marched onwards.

Years of having to tough out the last few miles had prepared me for this. I hadn't been rubbish at pacing it seemed, just practising for a race I never thought I'd be stupid enough to enter. At the checkpoint I popped my head in the door, got number checked and pushed on. This was all familiar but if I stopped I might not start again. I was managing to gain back more time and was pretty much on schedule. I'd planned 18min30 pace for this section which although hard on the hills, I can beat on the flats. After, I would only have eight miles left with two final climbs.

The climb to the hill overlooking the Old Man of Wilmington is basically evil. The surface is hard work, being uneven, rutted and lined in loose flints, and the hill loops back on itself with several false summits. Fortunately, in the dark you can't see these so, having resigned myself to nearly two miles of trudging climb, it didn't feel as awful as expected. The descent into Jevington for the final checkpoint was mentally tougher as I was passed a few times. Any places I'd gained on the climbs or flat were lost on the descents as my legs crashed heavily down and removed any benefit of gravity enjoyed by those with working legs. Despite this, I made time and, at the checkpoint, was not merely back on but ahead of schedule. Running the later stages of a race better than expected was a first for me and a shocking situation.

On the final climb I rang Cloë to wake her, knowing I needed a friendly face at the finish, and settled into the slog in the dark. Comedy entertainment was provided when a husband-and-wife team passed me. He'd run the route before but had promised this would be his last year. She was eagerly seeking witnesses to this fact: 'See, you told *him* you wouldn't run again.'

I then lost a couple more spaces to runners with cheat sticks (walking poles). I don't know how much they help, but the two seemed to glide past in a click-clack accompaniment. Pondering whether I should get poles next time, I realised that I was considering a next time. When did this happen?

Finally, I reached the Trig point overlooking Eastbourne. It's literally all downhill from here and I nearly kissed the marshal when I saw him. With two miles left, all I needed was to descend into the valley of death and run on some nice smooth pavement. The valley was worse than I remembered though. My legs were so heavy I couldn't even walk and was obliged to take a painfully slow stepping down method. Step, together, step, together, wedding march. Relieved by each successful step, I was like Granny leaving the pub after too many ports.

I got passed a lot. I lost count. Unsure how many were still in the race it seemed like the bulk of them were passing me in the penultimate mile.

After what felt like hours of hobbling slowly down a path I found a short road section before the overgrown alleyway. Any bit of exposed skin not already stung, burnt or scratched would be given one last chance here, before Willingdon Road. Having got lost here on the 50 I was keen to keep on route, and set off for the final flat mile back. Pretty sure I was on schedule, my brain was nonetheless foggy and I couldn't swear if I was about to break 24 or 23 hours. The sun peeking up suggested it was probably about 4.30am. Maybe.

I felt like walking. I walked. It felt good. I could walk the rest of the way. I could walk in and savour it, but if I got passed again I might throw myself under a bus. Passing the hospital (don't cut through, instant DQ the rules say), I closed on two runners. Focusing on them, I closed the gap and passed at a rate that would need time-lapse photography to discern.

Rounding the corner of the car park before the stadium I was greeted not just by Cloë (who received, I am confident to say, the sweatiest hug ever bestowed on a wife) but by Jen, her husband Andy, along with her two pacers, Julie and Dennis, who had all hung around after Jen finished (2.5hrs ago) to witness my shambolic running climax. Not wanting them to wait any longer I picked up my feet and, in a messy puddle of sweat, tears and snot, lapped the track for a 22h22m finish. In my head that last 400m was run quicker than Mo Farah on his closing lap of a 10,000m race. I must have looked like a man walking to the pub but with far more arm swinging.

Marathon 97 was done. It's a bloody hard way to get another notch and I still can't believe it. My legs did their best to remind me for the next few hours in bed where they simply ached in whatever position I tried to lie. If you've had toothache, imagine that from the waist down.

It was a great experience and I'd swung wildly from 'I

am never doing this again even if I don't finish' through to 'If I get sub 24 I won't have to do this again' and then breaking out into 'I wonder how much further or faster I could go if I did it again...' after which I sneeze and nearly pass out from the pain.

Somewhere in this post-run fog I started looking for other races. The Autumn 100 (also by Centurion Running) was scheduled for October that year. Being the race I briefly paced Chris at previously, and the event that opened my eyes to the world of ultra-running, I felt drawn. It was sold out but, as with the Chiltern Wonderland 50, I stuck my name on the waiting list and waited with hope and fear that I might get a place.

27

RACE SERIES

Some of the best running events I've taken part in have been the least publicised. Big city marathons crank the PR hard to get 30–40,000 runners to part with upwards of £60, but a local running club can sell out its £10 race on word of mouth alone.

Although Milton Keynes is a new city, it has a long history of running events and the *Tour of MK* has been going for decades, put on by Marshall Milton Keynes Athletic Club. When I took part in 2017, it was the 35th running. One of those under-publicised but amazing local events, it consists of six races over six days in and around MK, including everything from a track mile to a five-mile cross-country. It's a complete step down in distance for marathon runners but it's liberating not to worry about pacing and nutrition. Just run as hard as you can to finish sweat-drenched on a summer's evening then do it all again the next day. There's also the hope that some faster miles will make the autumn marathon events quicker.

In my case I was killing time between marathon 99 and the all-important 100. I'd left sufficient time to get some last-minute marathons completed should I fall behind schedule. I hadn't and faced the frightening prospect of many weeks with no races to compete in.

You can enter for individual days, but the real attraction is the full tour, competing against, and getting to know, each other in a (friendly) competitive spirit. Nothing will propel you onwards at the end of a hard race as much as 'Bob', who is level pegging with you on cumulative time, trying to slip past on the last bend.

Day 1 – Tattenhoe 11km (more like 10.8k)

The first day is possibly the hardest: a three-lap course around Tattenhoe, mixing wide redway footpath with narrower footpaths around the park. Predominantly flat, it enjoys some gentle ups and downs at underpasses. What makes it hard is the standard of the runners. All the fast boys and girls come out to play. You can't help but be swept along in the stampede and wonder why your lungs are making a bid for freedom a mile in.

Those runners that are in for the full tour need a good start, so everyone goes hard and, while not much longer than a 10k, that extra distance takes it from 'ouch this is hurting' to 'for the love of deity, when will it end?' My breathing felt fine but my quads did their best to remind me it was only a week since they were asked to push my weighty self around my 99th marathon and that they would appreciate a longer rest.

The end comes just after a bend as you turn off from the park so if, like me, you're not paying attention (and arguing with your legs) suddenly you're in the final sprint to the finish without realising it until other runners start to pass. For the first two laps you make a hard left and start your next lap, for the final lap you need to run on to the chip matt and welcome refreshments.

My own loss of time came by daydreaming in the final lap. I struggled to keep up and lost sight of those in front. My mind wandered to thinking how good it would be to stop and if it was going to be dry enough to cut the lawn when I got home, and I started to slow. Only a chance check of the watch reminded me I was meant to be racing and not out for a jog.

Day 2 – Potterspury Cross-Country 5 mile (more like 4.86 mile)

Day two meant rushing after work to a small village outside of MK. The route starts in a field with a mini lap before two main laps.

Although there is only 134ft of elevation gain the course never feels flat, and the stream crossings (five in total) and stiles to climb (four of them) combine with ascents across ploughed fields to earn the course its cross-country status. In most years someone will be flabbergasted by the streams and weep openly for their sodden trainers at the end.

The route is very runnable, and narrow footpaths give an interesting tactical element where overtakes, to be planned to get ahead of someone before the next stile, are weighed against the extra effort needed to run through long grass and nettles.

The final few hundred metres take you out of the stream crossing (mid-shin most years) to lap the playing fields. Once again, I was outsprinted and lost several places in the final section from my lack of a fast finish.

Day 3 – Stantonbury Track Mile (an actual 1 mile)

Yep, an actual timed mile on the track, done like a proper runner. Intimidating.

The runners are split into groups of similar ability based on current tour standings. This prevents a four-minute athlete having to lap a far slower runner, and aids competition. As runners should be able to keep up in their groups, they can work off each other.

For anyone who hasn't raced a track mile before, it's approximately 1.6km or four and a tiny bit laps of the 400-metre track. Unlike Usain Bolt in the 100 metres, they have no assigned lanes or starting blocks. Instead, a gently curved line is painted across the track just before the finish line, and that equates to one mile. Runners assemble shoulder to shoulder on the line and await the start gun. There follows something between an orderly fast procession to the first bend, or possibly a mass scrum.

For most recreational runners without a track

background, a standalone mile is ridiculously hard to pace. Start at a sprint and you quickly learn that a mile is a long way when you're already slowing on the first lap, and being passed for three more laps. If you go off too slow and get stuck behind others, it's frustratingly short. You're not at the Olympics so finish position doesn't count, but you need to make the best of what little speed your legs have. Running the shortest route in the quickest time requires some thought and practice. It's surprising how congested a track can feel with just a handful of runners. Overtaking on the bends requires you to run wide and cover more ground at a quicker pace. Mo Farah can do this.

I hate to break this to you, but you're not Mo Farah. Realistically, you need to keep overtakes for the straights. Given that the final straight will be a lung-busting everything-you've-got sprint finish, you only have seven opportunities to move up the pack and you'll likely waste the first couple trying to avoid being tripped or tripping someone else. On the bends, tuck in behind the runner in front and aim to hammer past coming out. The bad news is that the runner behind you has the same plan (and likely the one behind him too), so you end up in a three-way sprint, trying to beat the runner who came out the bend in front. Remember, he has a straight line to the next bend and therefore less to do.

For the stats nerds, going wide on the bend adds around three metres to the 100-metre length. Get stuck on the outside for every lap and you've added considerably to your race.

While cutting in and out trying to pass someone, you

deplete energy reserves at a rate you're not used to and your 'fast twitch muscle fibres', dormant during marathon training, will wonder what the hell is happening.

After four laps there is a sprint finish for the line when, typically, someone you fought to pass will glide ahead like an athletic puma, displaying perfect running form and poise, head held high, while attracting admiring looks from the spectators. By all means, swing your arms wildly around in the vain hope they will motivate your protesting legs to move faster, gurn like a cow sucking a lemon, and collapse over the line with as much grace as a sofa falling out of a tree.

Run the mile well and you will achieve a time you did not know you were capable of. Run it badly and you may be only marginally faster than your average mile time for a parkrun.

With all this in mind I lined up for the start, went like a bat out of hell for the first bend and found myself in the front group. Regret kicked in when I was caught and passed on both sides, which made it impossible to get back on the inside. If you drive on the motorway you'll doubtless have come across a car labouring in the middle lane, unable to keep up with the flow of traffic and being undertaken and overtaken by streams of vehicles blaring their horns. That was me in this race. Eventually I ran out of people to be overtaken by and spent two laps keeping my ill-advised, last-minute Red Bull down. In the final lap I tried to close the gap before the finish line.

My Garmin beeped somewhere on the final bend having over-read the distance, and I forgot to stop my watch, so only later did I learn that my finish time was

5:56. This was better than I'd managed before but, given a 6:05 first mile for a previous half marathon, hardly a massive leap.

Day 4 – Campbell Park 5 mile (more like 4.2 miles)

Legs recovered from the fastest mile they've ever done? No? Too bad, it's time for day four!

The race of two laps starts by the MK Rose, a weird sculpture sun dial installation. The first section is across the grass and down Beacon Hill in Campbell Park. Running downhill feels glorious but your brain will remind you the finish is a long way above you and you have two laps to go. The route is: redway to the Grand Union canal and along the towpath, before climbing back through Downs Barn on a long slow climb to the start of lap two. Repeat the route, divert off the path for the finish arch and a triumphant close drenched in sweat.

Pacing is hard as it's effectively a mile downhill and a mile uphill. You don't want to leave yourself nothing for the ups but take it too easy on the downs and you'll lose position. Being on the 'husky' side I went as fast as possible on the downs to gain some advantage. It probably wasn't the best move as my final mile was awful and I was passed multiple times. The runner next to me in the tour standings planned his race better and opened his 1 second advantage to well over a minute.

Day 5 – Brickhill Woods Hill Race (2.1 miles)

A two-mile run in the woods sounds pleasant. Don't be fooled. The route twists and turns around trees, up and down inclines, taking in some lovely off-camber sandy stretches that are either clinging muck or shifting dust depending on recent weather. There is little point in studying the route: just follow the runner in front and pay attention to the marshals and markings. Even if asked to run the route again immediately after the finish I doubt I'd be able to follow it without help. Run hard throughout, overtake if you dare and be prepared to finish after a mere two miles feeling broken. It's brilliant.

Timekeeping not being my best quality, I arrived later than planned, parked further away than I liked and did a fast warm-up run to reach the start. The runners were assembled on the relatively wide footpath but shoulder to shoulder. I employed my best jungle skills to hack through the undergrowth and burst out onto the path where I expected to finish in the pack.

It was a scrum when we set off, and a tight right to turn uphill, so I dived into the undergrowth and through bracken to gain a few spots and avoid being held up on the twisty sections. On the rest of the course there was little room for tactics as it became a mad scramble up, down and across the hills and ditches.

Competitors have no sense of how far they've run and have no opportunity to check their watches as every step needs concentration to avoid tripping, headbutting or impaling yourself on nature. On the few open sections they will be too busy making up ground. On other events

I tend to get distracted by my own thoughts, assessing how my legs feel, calculating distance to the finish and the pace required, but there's none of that here.

It's my favourite race of the tour as it doesn't feel like a race so much as a full effort sprint to escape a pack of zombies. It's less about passing the runner in front as putting as many people as possible between myself and the pursuing beast monster. Finally, without warning after innumerable descents, runners burst out of the undergrowth onto a tight left turn and sprint down a narrow path to the finish. It's all over and the nightmare pursuer has been evaded for another year.

This was my best performance of the series as I passed runners throughout and finished ahead of many who had consistently trounced me all week. I'd like to think this is due to athletic ability but can accept it had more to do with gravity.

Day 6 – Willen Lake 6 miles (more like 6.4 miles)

The final day of the tour! By now you know who's in competition with you on overall standings (or if you're really good, in contention for a position or age category award) and will be desperate to stay ahead. That gap you built up over five races could be wiped out on a bad day. Conversely, the lead the runner ahead of you has is unassailable and not worth even trying to close. It's probably the closest you'll get to being a *Tour de France* rider.

The race starts and finishes at the Woughton Sports

Pavilion, taking an out and back route to Willen Lake along the Ouzel valley park (a linear park following the river Ouzel between Willen and Caldecotte Lakes). One side of the river has wide uninterrupted footpaths (and passes by my house). The other side has grazing livestock and multiple cattle gates. For some reason the route follows the latter path, with some of the gates tied back while others are held open by volunteers who may not be there on the way back. With some though, it's for the runners to open as they approach at collision speed, praying the catch is oiled and free. For the adventurous (who don't wish to use their ankles anytime soon) there is the option of leaping the cattle grid in a single bound. This is best suited to long jump champs, but careful stepping across can be used by the sure-footed.

The gates all have their own quirks. When pushed hard, some will open wide and close slowly, allowing a fellow runner to nip through. Others pushed with the same force will bounce off the post and hammer back at wrist-snapping speed. The runner behind will likely think of you as a total arse and contemplate pushing you into Willen Lake before returning the same way.

The best bit about approaching the finish is the knowledge that the series is done and dusted and a buffet and tour tee shirt awaits.

Although I found the route OK, earlier rain made the paths slippery for my poor trainer choice and I found better grip on the grass alongside the path. Heading out, I stuck in a good pack and the gates were easy. Heading back, I was blowing out my arse and mostly left to flounder at the gates on my own, finishing 38th out of 105 full tour entrants.

The total mileage for the series is around 25 so for many, it is a low mileage week but *all hard*. There is a great atmosphere at all the races, and at £30 for the series (with a tech tee) or £5 per race, great value. No medals, no sports drink, no faff. Just run hard and drink water at the end.

28

THE MAGIC 100

About the 100 Marathon Club

There are many 100 marathon clubs across the world but, for anyone UK-based, the imaginatively named '100 Marathon Club' is the one to join. It also attracts a lot of overseas members due to its stringent rules.

There are various qualifying criteria on the website but, essentially, events must be organised, advertised marathons (or longer) with a race permit, a minimum number of race finishers, and published results. This is to ensure they are actual marathons and not a couple of mates going for a training run (or even a cycle) one evening and claiming it as a marathon. It upholds the integrity of the club and makes membership all the more worthwhile.

Other points to note are:

Relay events (part of a team running laps) don't count even if you ran over the 26.2 miles.

Ultras count for 'one', not multiples of 26.2miles. Any races you failed to finish, even after covering marathon distance, don't count as you're officially a DNF. Break your leg 99 miles into a 100 miler and you get nothing more than a cool cast and a great story to tell your mates.

The club has two levels of membership. Upon reaching 50 you can apply to join as an associate member by submitting a marathon count sheet provided on their website and having it vetted. Assuming you have 50+ valid marathons and sufficient road marathons, you can join as a 'Wannabe' while progressing to full membership.

Picking your 100th Marathon

By now you've become an approved associate member and have been tracking your marathons on the count sheet, making sure you get enough road marathons done and dusted to tick that particular box. It's time to start considering the milestone and the reason you started this adventure.

Your 100th marathon and how you mark the occasion are matters of choice. Some may want the milestone to pass quietly with just a few handshakes from friends. Others want to make more of a fuss.

Typically, members plan their final races and pick a target event in the future for their 100th, leaving enough scope between to pick up a few extra events should there arise a need to make up for any cancelled marathons or some missed due to injury or commitments.

Smaller events are often best for what you might see as 'your day'. You'll get a name check from the Race Director and support around the course from other runners. Run your 100th at London and you won't even get a mention unless you're a celebrity, and good luck trying to find a quiet pub with room to meet after. There is no reason not to pick an ultra as your 100th, but the wide range of finishing times means you might be celebrating with just the Race Director and some cows in a muddy field while waiting for your companions to finish.

With the event picked, check the 100MC website to make sure no one else has nominated that event. It's not the done thing to gate-crash someone else's 100th and steal their thunder. You've both run 2,620 miles and both deserve your own moment to shine. Let the club know of your planned 100th and submit your final count sheet up to and including your 100th marathon 12 weeks before the day for checking. Six weeks in advance, order your club gear, but allow longer if you want to send it away to get your name printed. You're now ready to go.

Countdown to the 100th

Given I'd run enough laps of Caldecotte Lake in Milton Keynes to have worn my own groove in the path, it was only fitting to pick an Enigma Running event for my

100th. After working through dates and planned events, I chose a September event. Hopefully it would not only be warm enough to enjoy some beers in the pub garden, but also allow enough time to fit some more in, given I had a 50 and a 100 miler planned with the real prospect of injury or DNF. It was only when I hit 95 marathons that it began to seem real.

I'd publicised it within the club and among other running friends, and Foxy had agreed to allow relay entry so those unable to commit to a full marathon could run a single lap and still earn the blinging medal. I was taken aback by how many wanted to join me; enough to form seven teams with names to reflect my running career. 'Awesome' and 'Man of Steel' would have been good, but 'Bleeding Nipples', 'Missed Team Photo', 'Late as Usual', and 'Piss-poor Pacing' were the predictable choices.

After finishing the 100 miler in June I was confident: only three marathons stood between me and the shirt. I placed the order for tee and medal and forgot about it until I opened the package a few days later, almost recoiling at the touch. I'm not superstitious, but had I just jinxed myself?

Calming down, I searched for somewhere to get my name printed on the top, so I could put it away and forget about it again.

Marathon 98 was an Enigma event and I ran to feel, not checking pace but just running at what felt sustainable, netting a 3h22m finish and my second fastest time. It felt good and, after the ultras, was a positive sign that I was getting my speed back. 99 was planned to be faster still, with my 100th goal being to better or match my 3h15m PB.

Two weeks in Italy prior to marathon 99 should have been ideal acclimatisation for an August marathon. Having consumed copious beer and pizza I arrived back late Saturday, ready to let rip on my penultimate marathon. On Sunday morning I bid farewell to my family, hello to the McDonald's staff for the pre-race ritual, and turned up ready for another seven and a bit laps of Caldecotte Lake.

My plan was to ignore the watch and, again, run to feel. This kept me in 1st place for over a lap before losing a spot, and then a couple of laps later I lost a further place as the temperature climbed. It wasn't as hot as Italy but hotter than predicted and was taking its toll. I'd forgotten a hat (bad planning) and my sunglasses collapsed somewhere around mile 16, either by the G-forces imposed by my early pace or because they got squashed in the suitcase on the flight back.

At 18 miles I struggled to keep below 8min/mile pace. It was now a challenge to hold on for 3rd place and 3h28m. Another sub 3h30m was in the bag, but not the improvement I'd been hoping for ahead of my 100th.

Running my 100th – Earning the shirt

Some finish lines are magical because of their location. Running down The Mall in London after waving at the Queen, and crossing the chip mat to be handed your medal is guaranteed to bring tears to the eye of even the most stoic runner. Push yourself to run further than you dreamed possible and, whether a 10k or a 100 miler, that gantry you pass under is a moment you won't forget. The mixture of heartache, exhaustion, relief and pride is palpable.

My significant finish was at a lake in Milton Keynes. The line was marked by a flag on the path, the course was marked with flour and there was a noticeable absence of chip mats, finish arches, enormous timing clocks, goody bags and other paraphernalia. The timing was done on a clipboard by a bloke called David, sitting on a chair in the sun. The medal was presented by the Race Director also called David, and live TV coverage via your red button was certainly not an option.

The finish was special because of the lack of unnecessary junk, pomp and ceremony, not despite it. I couldn't think of anywhere else I'd rather be for the culmination of six years of dogged persistence. The chance suggestion from school mate Dave had started something, and a chance meeting with a 100 Marathon Club member during my first (and I thought only) marathon had infected my common sense with a further idea.

I didn't dare verbalise it for fear of mockery, but I wanted that top.

On a chilly and damp Saturday morning in September I pulled on my tried-and-tested marathon kit like a professional. Extensive trial and error means I'm a sort of expert, or possibly an idiot for not listening to advice. After stopping at McDonald's for essential fuelling I left for Caldecotte Lake, but this time was different. This time it was my 100th and I'd be pulling on the hallowed

100 Marathon Club top that had motivated me through countless 5am training runs with snot freezing on my face and poorly designed running shorts doing their best to rub away that which I'd rather keep in place.

The turnout from the running club was amazing, with around 50 taking part to share the day with me. After being present for countless other marathon celebration events it was finally my day. Usually the bridesmaid, now the bride.

Foxy (another David), the Race Director, started the race and I was off for the final 26.2 miles of a 2,620 mile journey.

In each of the seven laps I was greeted by cheers and applause from ever increasing crowds gathered at the gazebo erected by another clubmate called David (there is a theme here) and expertly catered by my long-suffering but ever supportive wife Cloë. I had company for the laps and held a steady pace. Terry was running leg 1 for one of the relay teams and, despite returning from abroad only hours earlier, was a cheerful companion. We run together well. After 99 attempts I was thinking suicide pace is probably not the way to go and maybe this constant pace theory has some benefit.

Clubmate Stephen, fresh from a 185 mile run at King Offa's Dyke Race, kept a good pace from the start. I was delighted with his company but dismayed he can run a 7:20min/mile pace a mere four days after running for 74hrs with 'as much as two hours sleep a night'. Many say my love of running is excessive. Compared to Stephen I've barely started. Fortunately for my ego, he tired and dropped back after three laps, leaving me with never-tiring training buddy Jen, soon joined by Matt and Dennis.

Every time we passed the finish line I was surprised by yet another friend, work colleague or relative who had come to witness the awesome sight of a perspiring fat man living out a midlife crisis.

The boating club on the South Lake was holding a regatta and the 'fun' of dodging rowers who were comically swinging oars was lifted by the compere cheering us on and announcing 'Here comes the lead marathon runners'. I seized on it but I'm sure Eliud Kipchoge never had to negotiate an Olympic class coxless four crossing the race route while he was trying to break two hours for the 26.2 miles.

Going past halfway was on pace and in the lead. Although aware that this lofty position was due to other local races and a major marathon in Berlin, I was still happy to hold the spot. If I could hold the pace as well, I'd manage the trippy whammy of personal best, race win and 100th marathon.

Company came and went as friends joined me either as part of their long steady run or part of their faster session. All made sure to stay behind me, offering no physical support or aid, thus avoiding any suggestion of unofficial pacing. This was a race I did not want to be disqualified from.

From about mile 18 I start to fade, not unexpectedly. The weather was clearing and the temperature climbing. It was great for spectators, less so for runners. Marathon advice would recommend dropping a gel before this point and a few more on route to the finish, but experience has shown that my stomach will object and the rowers could find themselves sharing the lake with a half-digested Egg McMuffin. I stuck to sports drink and water, and clubmate Matt helped me focus and limit the fade.

On the penultimate lap I glanced back to see a runner gaining. The pace now made a PB look remote, but I really didn't want to lose 1st place.

Starting the final lap, one of the Davids (I genuinely can't recall which) rang the bell to the cheers of a sizeable crowd. The next time I attract so many well-wishers and acquaintances to one place will probably be my funeral. What a cheerful thought for mile 23.

Focus. Only 3.5 miles stood between me and the hefty medal. And a beer. I really want a cold beer, as that will mean I've finished and can stop running. I briefly considered stopping for a quick one but one of the many people called David reminded me that the second-placed runner was gaining, so I took water from the table and pushed on.

I lost Matt when he agreed to accept 'carry my dog back duty', after she saw me running and decided to join in the final lap. Bella is well used to running with me, could handle the pace better than I, but couldn't understand why, this time, she wasn't allowed due to race rules.

This final lap is now just me, the clock, and a runner in orange creeping up behind me. He kept me honest; there could be no letting up. The twisting nature of the course offered few opportunities to gauge the closing runner's progress. The presence was more felt than seen, like the alien in a science fiction film with limited budget for special effects.

Counting off the way-markers as I passed them for the final time (goodbye stinky dog bin, adios trip-trap troll bridge, farewell regatta people and your massive pile of abandoned shoes), I found myself on the home stretch. Catching up with clubmates Connor and Emma on their long training run, I turned the final corner and pushed for the finish line. They may not have been as numerous as the London crowds, but the assembled masses were a more welcome sight. I crossed the line a fraction under 3h18m and opted for a little lie-down on the grass. I'd finished, and won, only narrowly missing the personal best that really would have been the cherry on the icing of the sweetest cake. I wasn't disappointed. There will be other PB attempts, but I'll only have one 100th marathon.

2,134 days since my first marathon. 2,620 marathon miles (and a few more for some ultras). Close to 12,000 total miles run since I started. I was finally done.

The first beer was thrust into my hand by Cloë and I started to celebrate, engulfed in a whirlwind of back slaps, kisses and firm handshakes. It was not unlike our wedding, wanting to spend time with everyone and thank them for coming but always needing to move onto the next group of people. School mates were sharing beer with running clubmates. Even the two factions of Lakeside and Redway Runners were mingling and avoiding a West Side Story rival club dance-off.

The kids seemed bemused to see Daddy being the centre of attention when they'd long since stopped being impressed by 'sweaty Daddy with bleeding boobies'.

Our friend Victoria has made an amazing cake of the 100 Marathon Club top which was almost too perfect to cut. And of course Dave 'fancy a jog' was there to see the final culmination of quite how far I'll go when given a good suggestion on a wet February evening. By now I figure he owed me at least a few pair of trainers.

The beer flowed and eventually it was time for Foxy as RD to perform the presentation. During the speech he remarked that more people have climbed Everest than run 100 marathons. I suspect more people have climbed Everest than smashed themselves over the head with a frying pan 100 times too. I'd joined a small club of gluttons for self-inflicted punishment and finally pulled on the top I'd spent so long chasing. It was a bit itchy to be honest.

Still, 100 marathons. Not bad for a fat lad.

29

WHAT'S NEXT?

Having knocked out 100 marathons and some decent ultras where do I go from here? A good question.

I not only want to keep running, but need to in order to keep myself broadly in shape – although of course inactive Mark would be a shape: a big round globe. If I keep the miles up I maintain a normal body shape. However, I doubt I'll ever reach the dizzy heights of 'normal' on the Body Mass Index (BMI) system as running has given me legs that could kick-start a jumbo jet and skinny jeans are something other people wear.

My first goal is to get fast enough to qualify as Good for Age in the London Marathon, as much to feel I am actually good at running as to take part in the event again. I'd also like to complete the Abbott World Marathon Majors, a series consisting of six of the largest and most highly regarded marathons in the world. It was five until Tokyo was added in 2013. The full list is Tokyo – Japan, Boston – USA, London – UK, Berlin – Germany, Chicago – USA and New York – USA. Although not a cheap undertaking, doing the full set earns you a 'Six Star' finishers' medal and certificate. Entry procedures vary: being fast or rich would be an advantage.

Then there's the Marathon des Sables. Often described as the 'toughest footrace on Earth' this is a multi-day ultramarathon set in the Sahara desert. It takes place over six days and entrants cover 251 km (156 mi) a similar distance to six normal marathons. What makes it stand out, other than the heat (up to 50°C) and sandy terrain is the need to be self-sufficient, carrying all your own food, clothing and equipment for the six-day fun run as well. The other unique aspect of the event is the price at around £4,500. Maybe a few years of being a very good boy or girl will be needed for Santa to reward you.

There are any number of great races I'd like to attempt. The Western States 100 is the original 100 miler. An unforgiving ultra through California's Sierra Nevada Mountains, started when a competitor in a horse race left his transport at home and ran it. Competitors take in burning sections in the valley and snow at the summits. The Comrades 'Marathon' is actually a 56 mile ultra, established in 1921. Every May 20,000 runners descend on South Africa to run the course as it alternates annually from the 'up' run (Durban to Pietermaritzberg) or the 'down' run (Pietermaritzberg to Durban). The race has a hard 12-hour cut-off as part of its charm. The last runner to make the distance and the first to fail to make the cut-off will both achieve their 15 minutes of fame and notoriety.

On the opposite end of the scale from Comrades sits The Barkley Marathons. An ultramarathon held in Frozen Head State Park near Wartburg, Tennessee, USA. Competitors are typically around 40 per year and finishers rare, with only 18 making it to the end in the 20-year history.

Running Mojo

The enjoyment of running will ebb and flow as you progress, or at least it certainly does for me. The early stages may feel like you're making no improvement and wasting everyone's time, but remember that however slow you're going, you're still lapping those at home on the couch.

The typical sedentary adult is not going to be the next Mo Farah or Paula Radcliffe without a lot of training and a lucky draw in the DNA raffle. Even with unlimited time and money you probably won't ever win a race, but that's not a reason to stop. The goal is to be a better you, not to qualify for the Olympics and set world records.

Every Sunday league football player past their early teens knows they'll never walk out at Wembley, but they still yearn to be part of their sport and to improve. Ultimately, you're only racing yourself, even if it some-times feels like you've kicked your own arse.

Early runs will stress your body and it will ask you to stop. Later, it will insist. Persist by ignoring these voices and push on even when the easy option is to get out of the rain, into the warmth of the house and snuggle on the sofa. Eventually these voices will fade and you'll enjoy the simple act of moving forward.

Much has been written about our anatomy and how we are literally born to run but instinct is something that modern life can knock out of us. Reconnecting with the basic need to get a sweat on and push is as close to spiritual mumbo jumbo as I'm ever likely to preach, but I know that for many of us some selfish 'me' time, where we cease to be colleague, mum, son, parent or partner, running with our own thoughts is the highlight of the week. It also helps us be better when we shed our soggy Lycra and return to being dad or wife.

I've been very goal-oriented throughout my running, first to complete longer distances, then to achieve better times. Improvement has never been linear. Periods of massive improvement and effortless PBs were usually followed by runs where legs were heavy, I felt like a broken packet of biscuits and my target pace was a laughable prospect in the distance.

When this happens to you, don't run home and burn your trainers and sports bra. Instead, indulge in the very un-British act of self-congratulation. You're now turning out distances and paces that you didn't even contemplate when you started. An awful run now would have split your head open from excessive smiling previously. As a runner you're at least 10 per cent more awesome than a non-runner.

Remember that, and keep at it.

www.sandstonepress.com

 facebook.com/SandstonePress/

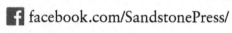 @SandstonePress